A CAPPELLA WARM-UPS

FOR POP AND JAZZ CHOIRS

BY DEKE SHARON & J.D. FRIZZELL

Online Exercises for this book are stored in the Hal Leonard My Library and may be viewed/streamed from that location or downloaded to your computer or tablet.

Log on to **www.halleonard.com/mylibrary** and enter the unique code below.

Once you have set up your secure account, you may access these files at any time and from any device connected to the internet.

To access Media files, go to:
www.halleonard.com/mylibrary

Enter Code
6474-3055-1142-1944

I0803437

ISBN 978-1-49-507741-8

HAL•LEONARD®
A Muse Group Company

Visit Hal Leonard Online at
www.halleonard.com

World headquarters, contact:
Hal Leonard
7777 West Bluemound Road
Milwaukee, WI 53213
Email: info@halleonard.com

In Europe, contact:
Hal Leonard Europe Limited
Dettingen Way
Bury St Edmunds, Suffolk, IP33 3YB
Email: info@halleonardeurope.com

In Australia, contact:
Hal Leonard Australia Pty. Ltd.
4 Lentara Court
Cheltenham, Victoria, 3192 Australia
Email: info@halleonard.com.au

Table of Contents

SECTION I: PREPARATION

SECTION II: THE WARM-UPS

POP

Jazz

Warm-ups by Skill

Rhythm

Syllables

Tone

Intervals

Dynamics

Intonation

Blend

Balance

PITCH

IMPROVISATION

SOLO

VOCAL PERCUSSION

Section I: Preparation

WHY WARM UP?

Everyone warms up before they play sports or exercise...right? Well, they should, as those who don't have a higher risk of injury. Muscles require stretching, range of motion, and gradual increase in blood flow to operate efficiently. In addition to the physiological aspects of warming up, most athletes also have some kind of pre-workout ritual—a way to focus their mind and emotions, priming them for optimal performance.

Singing is a fundamentally physical activity. Your body requires the use of many muscles to create a focused, high quality sound. We have to prepare our vocal folds so they are ready for the demands of our music, regardless of style. When singing, we engage the diaphragm, the intercostals, and even the muscles on our sides and around to our back. We have to focus our eyes to read the written page and to observe our fellow singers. We use the muscles in our ears to be more aware of tone, intonation, blend, balance, dynamics and articulation.

With this book, we've attempted to provide a wide array of warm-ups specifically designed for pop and jazz choirs, but these warm-ups will work well for contemporary a cappella groups of all sizes and styles. Don't look at this book as something that should be read straight through like a work of fiction; feel free to jump around and use various warm-ups as needed. Every vocal ensemble has its strengths and weaknesses which vary from year to year. The warm-ups within can help polish your weak spots and hone your strengths. Regardless of where your group's strengths lay, this book can help you address the full range of skills required for great music making.

I'll be honest, I very rarely warm up voices in my professional ensembles. It's not that I don't see any value, it's simply that the deadline always looms and time is short, be it on television, movies or Broadway. As a result, I tell my singers to arrive with their voices warmed up, which might mean 45 minutes of vocalizing for a soprano, and 45 seconds for a bass (life is unfair). However, what I will do is work on a variety of exercises with them, based on what they need to improve, be it blend, rhythm, phrasing or style. To this end, I'm not warming up voices, I'm warming up the ensemble. Over the years I've developed a variety of different short pieces, some drawn from my arrangements and original songs, that are specifically designed to focus a group's attention on one specific aspect of their singing. — Deke

I'll admit it, I'm a warm-up nerd. There. I said it. In the interest of full disclosure, though, I haven't always been a fan of warm-ups. For a long time, I rushed through them as fast as possible in order to start rehearsing music. After all, that's why my singers enrolled in choir, right? Over time, I began to realize that warm-ups could do so much more than simply warm up the physical voice. They also improve articulation, dynamics, phrasing, vowels, intonation, blend, balance and tone. They focus the ensemble, separating them from the day's distraction and removing the barriers to expressive, emotional, and connected singing. — J.D.

Rehearsal Procedures

When you enter the locker room of a professional sports team, it's an impressively organized space, with a specific place for everything and a number of clear procedures that the athletes all follow to ensure their time together is smooth and efficient. Similarly all types of vocal groups should have various procedures in place for their rehearsals, whether they are a glee club, show choir, jazz choir or contemporary a cappella group. These procedures should be understandable, repeatable and efficient.

We recommend you consider the following aspects of rehearsal, as a little attention and care can go a long way toward setting the right tone and creating a maximally productive rehearsal environment.

1. **Entry and Exit.** The manner in which singers enter and exit your rehearsal space each time they rehearse sets the tone and reinforces expectations for the time you'll spend together.

   Do you want them to grab their folder and pencil from a specific place? Should they be already warming up their voices as they enter the room? Do you want them socially interacting as a transition from other stresses of their day, or is too much talking in rehearsal an issue so you ask them to enter quietly?

   When rehearsal is over, what should singers do with their music – take it with them or file it? Who cleans up the stray papers, folders, pencils, water bottles and the like? Is someone in charge of stacking chairs or folding up risers?

   By making sure your expectations are clear and consistent, you can set the tone for a productive rehearsal while minimizing frustration and misunderstandings.

2. **New Music.** How do you generally introduce a new piece of music to your group? If you have printed sheet music, perhaps you insert the chart into their folders or place the music on the piano. If your singers use e-readers or tablets, do you email the music the night before, or upload it (Dropbox and Google Drive are good, free options) and expect them to download it themselves?

   Once the music is delivered to singers, how do you begin teaching it? Do singers gather around the piano to work on parts, or do you first have them divide and work in their sections? Either way, the goal should be to learn the notes and rhythms as accurately and efficiently as possible, with dynamics and phrasing as well as emotion baked in right away. From the very beginning, each time you read through a section of relatively unknown music without instruction on phrasing, dynamics, articulation, vowel shapes and diction, habits form.

   One trap we see far too often for pop and jazz choirs is having an entire choir learn notes and rhythms together, gathered around a piano while the director attempts to bang out one part at a time. This can be a very slow and painful way to learn a new tune. Many singers sit idle. Others inevitably learn parts incorrectly because the polyphonic nature of many a cappella arrangements makes it difficult for the director to play them simultaneously.

There's a much more efficient method: make practice tracks. The easiest way to do this is with a MIDI (instrumental) exported from your notation program: Finale, Sibelius, MuseScore, etc. Turn each voice part into an instrumental practice track by setting the playback instrumental sound to piano, synth brass, or strings[1]. Turning the MIDI volume up to around 120 for the active part while keeping the other parts around 60 helps your singers hear their notes. Better yet, pan the predominant part to the left channel and the others to the right, so your singers can learn their part by having one ear in, practice with everyone, and then remove their left ear and practice in a "music minus one" environment.

More time consuming but potentially more effective, sung practice tracks allow your singers to hear their part performed by a real singer (often you or the arranger). The advantage to this is that you can model tone, syllables, articulation, dynamics, vowel shape and phrasing in the practice tracks. The best way to make these is with a powerful yet expensive program called Melodyne Studio, which allows you to quickly tune and quantize (align pitch and rhythm). Software like Audacity and GarageBand are good, less expensive alternatives. To ensure accuracy, record each track with the full arrangement's MIDI in your ears as a guide. Start with the bass and work your way up. Be sure to tune the parts pretty aggressively, as you don't want singers learning out of tune notes.

3. **Starting warm-ups.** Who begins the rehearsal? Perhaps the director steps onto a podium, starts playing warm-ups on the piano or claps a four-beat pattern for their choir to echo back. These are clear signals, letting your singers know when they should begin focusing their energies on the musical task at hand. If your signal is understood, singers should engage immediately or the rehearsal dynamic is set and you'll likely have to frequently remind them to stop talking and focus. Every minute wasted on crowd control is a minute less of music making.

4. **Transitioning into rehearsal.** Once warm-ups are finished, how do you start your first piece of music? One strategy is to have the rehearsal plan on a chalk or white board for all to see. Another is to hold up the first chart to show your choir as you're completing the last warm-up. You could be really clever and end your last warm-up in the key of your first piece. The intent is to avoid announcing the piece and page while your choir spends a minute talking and getting out their music.

[1] Creating a stark contrast in texture between the active part and the other parts can help. Consider using piano for the other parts and synth brass or synth strings for the active part.

POP/JAZZ VS. CLASSICAL

One of the most common questions we're asked is: "How can I teach a pop (or jazz) ensemble if all of my training is in classical choral pedagogy?" We understand the concern, but the fact is there's little need to worry. Everything that you've learned in school pertains to contemporary musical styles, from the way you approach teaching a piece of music to the ways in which you should polish it for performance, with only a few exceptions:

1. **Vibrato is less present in popular idioms than in classical choral music.** Yes, there are times to add a little "spin" and no, you don't necessarily want all of your singers to be singing straight tone at all times, but the large, wide sound that you hear in the fourth movement of Beethoven's Ninth is too much. Listen to some popular a cappella groups to get a sense of the right amount, and where it's placed (usually only at the end of lines and during long held notes).

2. **Vowels tend to be more relaxed.** In general, a song should sound somewhat like contemporary speech, just as the lead vocals and background harmonies do on the radio. This might sound to your trained ear as lazy singing or loose vowels, but if you approach a current hit song with perfectly placed tall vowels, your choir will sound a bit like the King's Singers when they sing the Beatles: lovely but a tad anachronistic, especially if you have a younger ensemble. When singing homophonic textures, however, vowel unity is still important.

3. **Conductors do their work before the performance.** This is our polite way of saying that unless your group is very large (over 100 singers) or performing a piece with a great deal of rubato, you should prepare them in rehearsal to perform without you if at all possible. Popular music is by definition the people's music, and is best when the connection between the singers and audience is immediate, without "all eyes on the conductor!" Some of you may breathe a sigh of relief, others might find your ego bruised, but either way it should be clear: the performance is the result of your hard work, but it's not about you. Let the music and your singers do the work, and proudly accept applause afterwards.

4. **Rules don't apply.** This is our way of saying that even if something appears to be "wrong" according to your education, if it sounds good, then do it. The one major caveat is that your singers should never do anything to harm their voices, such as prolonged yelling. So long as they're not damaging their vocal chords, you're good. Yes, this means sometimes they'll swoop up to notes, sing breathily, or moments might be a tad sloppy or out of tune, as they are in the original recording. This is because, above all, in popular music emotion is supreme. Technique matters, but not to the exclusion of an audience's experience. If this goes against your instincts as an educator, think about the songs you loved growing up. Think about Motown: decidedly out of tune much of the time by today's standards, yet absolutely beautiful, compelling and joyous. Sometimes imperfection is, in fact, perfect.

5. **Tone varies by style.** Most of us have an "ideal" of what perfect choral tone is, whether that be the full, rich sound of Westminster Choir College, the warmth and homogeneity of St. Olaf, or the aggressive beauty of professional European choirs. If we're being honest with ourselves, there is no "perfect" choral tone—we all have our biases and preferences. The same concept applies to pop styles: A lighter, brighter, and airier tone for jazz. A darker, warmer tone for R&B. A more forward and full tone for Top 40. A more focused and enunciated sound for Broadway, exaggerated diphthongs in doo-wop and so on. We'll discuss tone in more detail in the next section with the help of Dr. Erin Hackel.

Value of Warming Up in Harmony

One of the best things about warming up is that it prepares the mind as well as the voice to have a productive rehearsal, as the day's thoughts are set aside. One of the worst things about warming up is that it can inadvertently train singers to "zone out" while they sing scales, resulting in an increased tendency to sing in "autopilot" mode while in rehearsal and on stage. When a group is warming up in harmony they are required to listen and focus on one if not several aspects of their singing, transforming the warm-up process from potentially passive to consistently active.

In addition, harmony singing is like anything else: the more you do it, the more natural it becomes. Locking chords, matching vowels, phrasing as a unit: all of these are the vocal equivalent of flying in formation, like the Blue Angels. The ear becomes attuned to hearing the vocal line as part of the whole, and the singer learns to focus on everyone else's notes, not their own. Good vocal harmony technique becomes instinctual, allowing the conscious mind to focus on the lyrics, the emotional content of a song, and connecting with the other singers on stage and the audience, as they should.

Teaching Your Singers to Sing in All Styles

By Dr. Erin Hackel

I have had the pleasure of working with Dr. Erin Hackel on several occasions: she's worked with my group OneVoice, I've worked with her group MIX, and together we've taught a three-day intensive on directing a cappella groups called Next Level (thevocalcompany.com). Not very many people impress me as much as Erin does. She has developed a method of teaching in non-classical settings that is poised to revolutionize the vocal pedagogy world. In 20 minutes, she had me belting notes I had only ever dreamed about hitting. No discussion of warming up voices for pop singing would be complete without her explanation of her techniques to you to start implementing with your groups. –J.D.

I am a classical singer, and proud to be one. I love opera, art song, oratorio, and don't even get me started on classical choral music. As I worked my way through three classical vocal degrees, I found that I was perfectly prepared to train other classical singers, maybe even classic musical theater singers. But soon I was plunged into an environment where I was expected to train contemporary singers. Singers who wanted to sing anything BUT classical music.

So I set off to find the tools I needed to teach these voices; specifically, I was looking for the same broad base of pedagogical knowledge that I had been given access to during my many years of classical voice and pedagogy study. To my dismay, what I found was: not much. Certainly nothing that approached the level of insight and research devoted to classical vocal techniques. Most of what I found was highly subjective, and not at all informed by research, anatomy, physiology or any pedagogical knowledge. Worst of all, I encountered an enormous bias from the classical voice community about contemporary singing.

I have spent the last decade turning my own knowledge of the voice and voice pedagogy to learning how to teach contemporary singers to sing in a healthful, sustainable way. It is my hope to pull back the curtain that shrouds vocal technique for every style of singing. To demystify the voice, and help teachers and singers really understand their voices and sing in any style they wish.

PART 1

Many books have been written on the workings of the muscles of our body, and exactly how our voices work, but we are here for clarity, not for an in depth scientific explanation. In broad strokes, we can say that the larynx, a series of cartilages and muscle, houses the vocal folds, which vibrate over air flow to make sound. The vocal folds sit horizontally over our wind-pipe, or trachea. When they are open, air passes through silently. When they close, they vibrate over the air and we make sound.

The Larynx and Vocal Folds

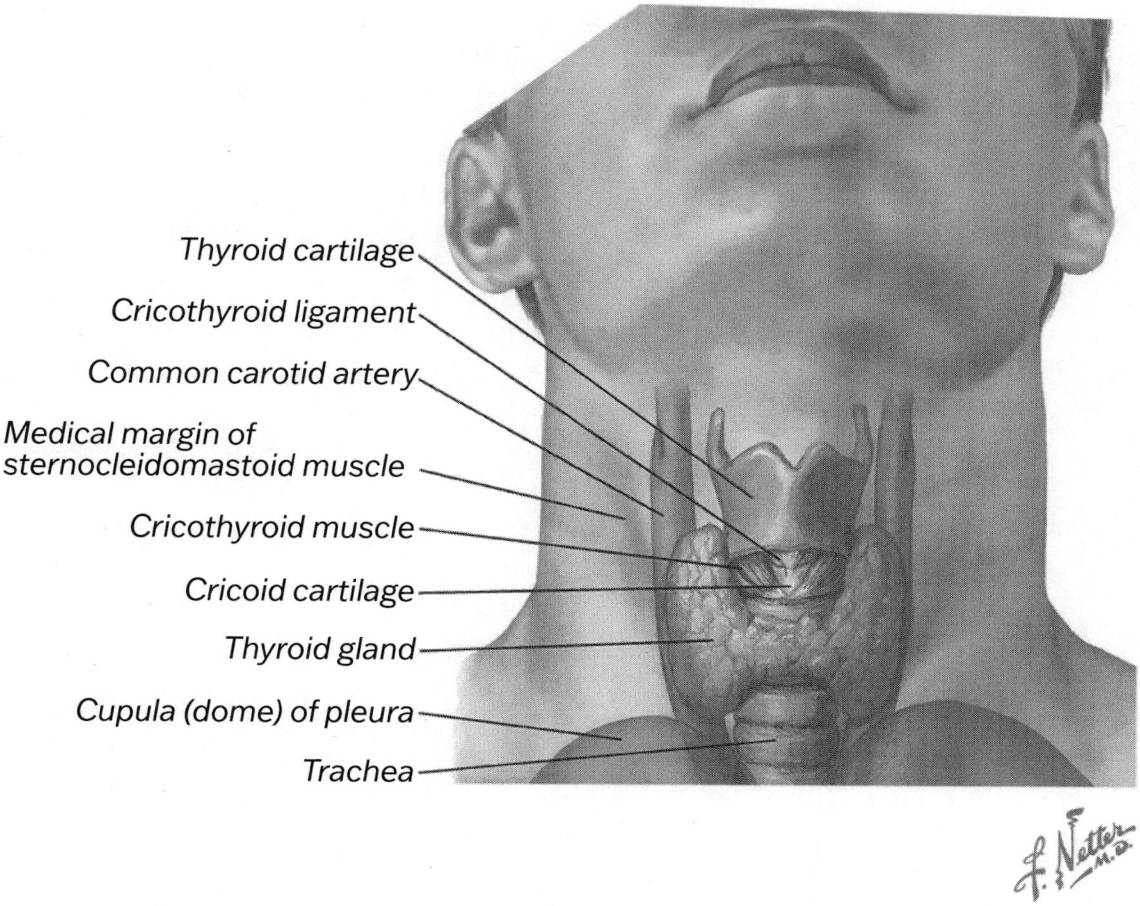

The Vocal Folds

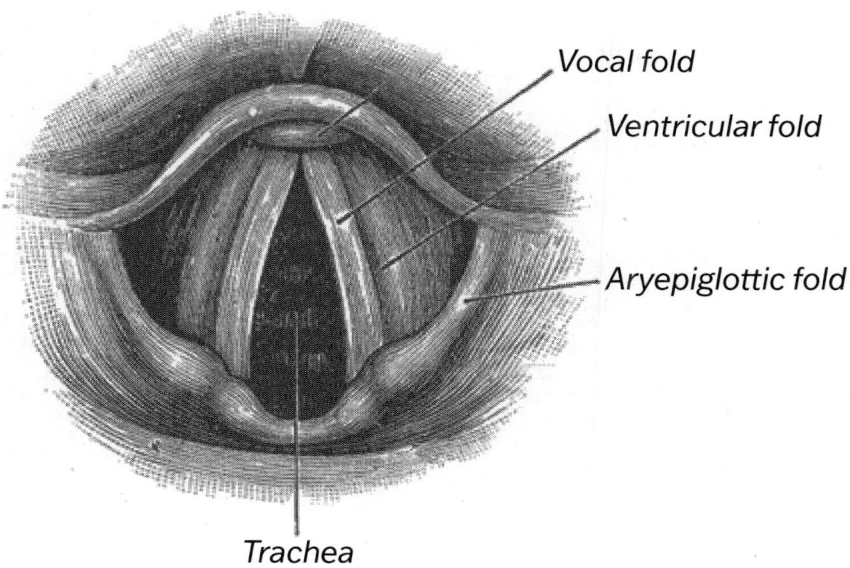

Singing is physical work. Our bodies must be fully engaged for a clear, present and active tone to be produced. Why? Think of it this way: the vocal folds can and will close and vibrate over whatever kind of air flow you give them. If you are seated, slumped over and sing, you will get one type of sound, probably quite thin and unstable. If, however, you maximize the vocal folds' abilities and give them an abundance of regulated air-flow, you will get a much higher quality sound. So, one of our goals is a strong, regulated air-flow. Here's how to achieve it.

Stand, with feet hip-width apart with a slight bend to the knees. Your sternum should be lifted, but not overly so; no need to pinch your shoulder blades. Alternately, you should not collapse your shoulders forward; your chest and back should feel like to equal halves of an oval. Breathing should feel easy and natural, with the abdominal muscles relatively relaxed.

Once our body is lined up, it's time to find some support for the regulated air-flow we desire. Remember: if the body collapses, our air-flow collapses. One of the best ways to keep the body engaged is to activate our epigastrium. The epigastrium is a region of the abdominal muscles that, when activated, pop out slightly. Find your epigastrium by placing two fingers right below the bottom-most bone of the sternum and coughing. It should tense quite a bit and pop out from your body. Practice holding that group of muscle out as you speak. As you sing, the epigastrium should remain out—this will also help your lower ribs to remain expanded, another key to good singing support.

The Epigastrium

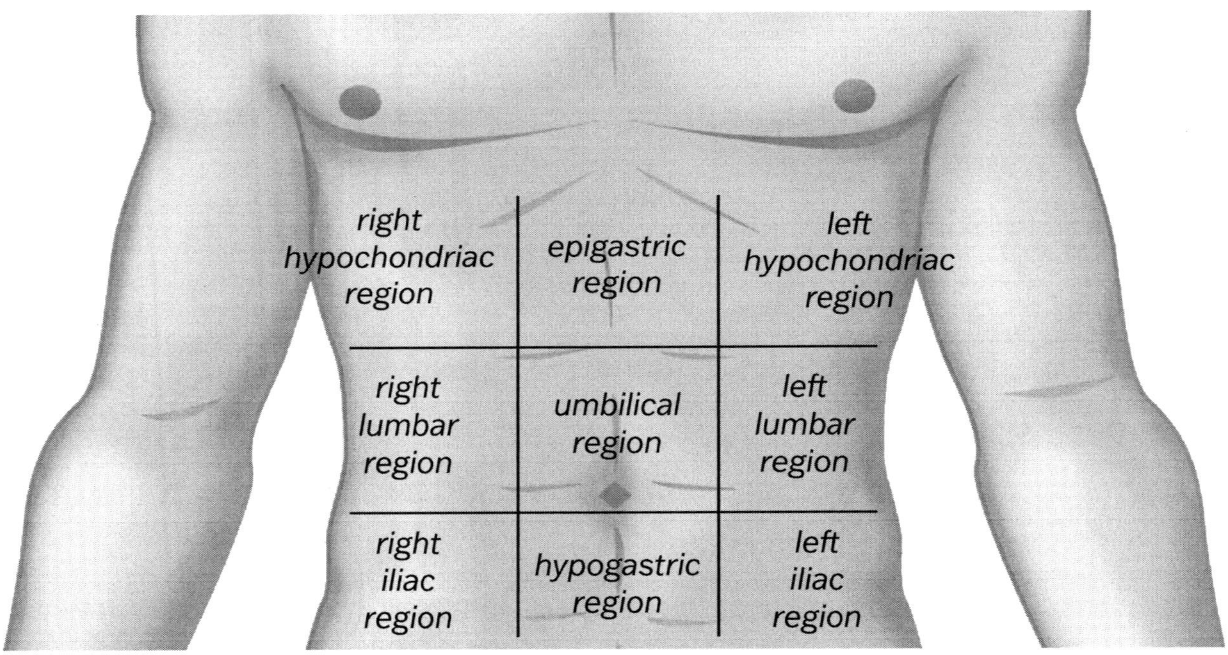

Now, rest your other hand over your lower abdominals. Here is where we create our regulated air-flow. With the epigastrium out, the lower ribs out and the upper sternum raised, sing a long, single tone while slowly pulling in the lower abdominals. Practice this oppositional movement on a sustained "shhhh" sound. Once these systems are in place, you are ready to create the optimal conditions for your vocal folds to do what they do best.

PART 2

Let's go back to the larynx. Place your fingers on your larynx and swallow. That's right, it moves. The larynx is not at all fixed like a bone, but slung between depressor and elevator muscles; it can and does move quite a bit. This is essential knowledge for singers, because the vertical position of the larynx completely alters the way you sound. For starters, the longer the tube, the lower the pitch. So it makes sense that you would lower your larynx to make richer, lower sounds. Think of watching a bass try to reach their lowest note—oftentimes they tuck their chin down. When they do that, they are trying to push their larynx down to make a longer tube and a lower note. Alternately think of a tenor trying to reach their highest note—they might lead with their chin and stretch their necks. They are trying to raise their larynx to make a shorter tube. It's instinctual. Becoming a master of the vertical positions of the larynx is key to unlocking the possibilities of your voice.

ANCHORED POSITION: CLASSICAL, OPERA, ART SONG

Position 4, the anchored position is the lowest possible laryngeal placement. Practice speaking in the anchored position in different volumes. You might think of this as your low, calm voice. Find a sustained pitch around C4 to sing while keeping your larynx in anchored position. You can use position four in all parts of your range to create a certain depth and warmth to the sound. Anchored position is used for classical and operatic singing in both men and women.

EASY POSITION: JAZZ, CLASSICAL MUSICAL THEATER, FOLK

Position 3, easy position is where your larynx naturally sits. It is probably where you use your speaking voice. Practice this position in different volumes at different pitch levels. This laryngeal position allows for dynamic range possibilities with just a bit more point to the voice, and is used by many jazz and folk singers. Most classical music theater is sung in position three.

ENERGIZED POSITION: POP, R&B, CONTEMPORARY MUSICAL THEATER

Position 2, energized position is just a half inch or so higher than the easy position. Find it by smiling, squinting as if the sun is in your eyes and speaking in a loud, perky voice. Or, think of a whiny child. The energized position is the perfect (and only!) position for belt voice singing. If you aren't in this position, you won't be able to sound like a pop or contemporary musical theater singer.

HIGH POSITION: SCREAMO ROCK, CARTOON VOICES

Position 1, high position is the highest point you can fix your larynx. It creates a very short tube, which is one way to access higher notes. The resulting sound is thin and high, and not used very much in mainstream singing.

Practice the vertical positions of the larynx by singing sustained pitches on or near C4 in all four positions. Notice how drastically different the sound is, just from this gross motor movement. Using these alone can make a classical choir sound like a pop choir, and vice-versa. Utilizing a variety of positions throughout a piece can make striking contrasts that will be accessible to all singers in a group. In solo singing, you will find that multiple laryngeal positions are used by many singers in contemporary styles, to create a mixture of warmth at the bottom of the voice to a more strident presence at the top.

PART 3

One of the most difficult parts of being a singer, or a teacher of singers, is that every part of the instrument is internal. The next section is going to require your visualization skills, as well as a willingness to sound, well, ugly. You will need to in order to get to know what's going on inside the larynx with your vocal folds.

The vocal folds are complicated structures, made up of layers of muscle and mucous; a whole book chapter could be written about them and their function (and has been, many times!), but we are here to simplify and clarify. The vocal folds vary in size between children, women and men, but they are very tiny – about .75-inch long in women and 1.0-inch long in men. They vibrate together very, very quickly– 60 times per second for a low pitch, up to around 2,000 times per second for a very high one. Each miniscule puff of air that escapes from each vibration is the beginning of a sound wave.

Thyroarytenoid and Cricoarytenoid Muscles

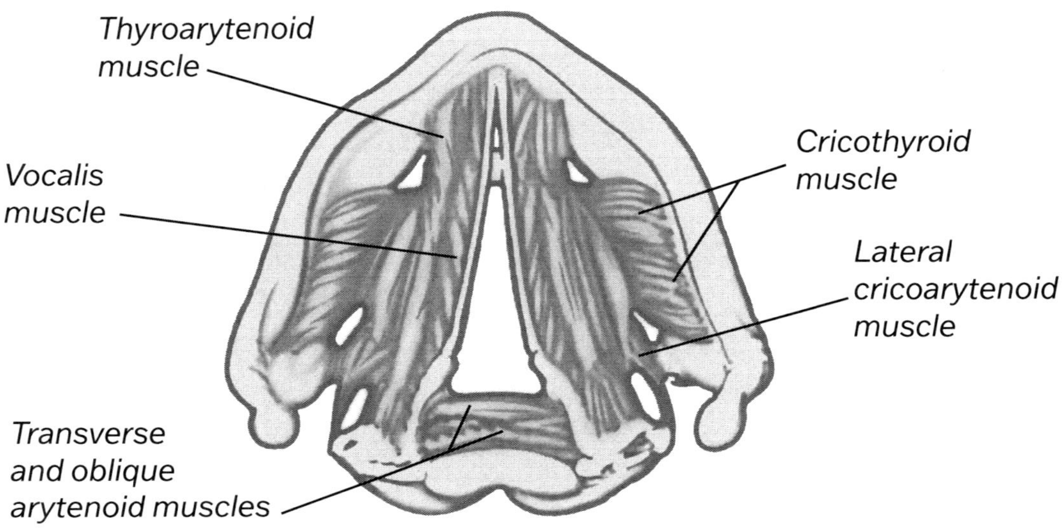

Here's the interesting thing: we can close the vocal folds using two different sets of muscles, and each of those will produce a drastically different sound.

The main body of your vocal folds has a muscular element to them; they are called the thryo-arytenoid muscles. I'll call those TAMs from here on out. The TAMs are very strong and able to close the vocal folds quite firmly over airflow. When they work alone, this is probably what you know as your chest voice or heavy mechanism. Practice isolating your TAMs by singing a low pitch as loudly as you can. Here's an important piece of information: using TAMs alone and taking the pitch higher will cause a singer to crack. If you are cracking around A4, man or woman, you are probably using only TAMs. TAMs are extremely strong in most male singers, and are especially developed in male operatic singers.

There is another way to close your vocal folds. Notice in the picture how the vocal folds form a "v" shape. At the open portion of each point of the "v," toward the back of your neck, are a set of smaller muscles called the cryco-thyroids. We will call them CTMs from now on. The CTMs are a wonderful group of muscles because unlike the TAMs, they allow your vocal folds to stretch over the air-flow. Remember how a high larynx/short tube can make a high sound? So can stretched out vocal folds. The CTMs are the sound of women's head voice or light mechanism, and men's falsetto. Practice this muscle function by singing a very light C5 on an [u] vowel. Notice how the sound is often lighter and breathier. This is because the CTMs are often overlooked and underdeveloped, especially in contemporary singers. Actually, the most common group of singers that seriously develop their CTMs are classical, operatic women. Their CTM function is extremely strong and allows them to sing very high and very loudly.

Developing your CTM is crucial to being able to sing in all styles. Why? Because the majority of contemporary singing is actually sung by using some combination of the two muscle functions. That's right. I'm talking about mixed voice singing, belting, voix mixte, or one of many other words. It all comes down to using these two groups of muscles, the TAMs and the CTMs on a spectrum. I've outlined the vocal fold spectrum next.

If we think about the intrinsic, or interior function of the vocal folds as being on a spectrum, we can isolate each position and master them independently. Once we have that down, we can purposefully decide which vocal fold position we wish to use to achieve a certain sound, whether it be for the duration of a piece, or for a portion of a piece.

Neutral/Fourth Gear

Rebecca Newman, English Soprano, 2008

The neutral position uses only the CT muscle. It is the falsetto in men and head voice in women. The neutral position is used almost exclusively in the classical female voice (except in a lower range), both in operatic and choral singers. It is used exclusively by male falsettists. The vertical position of the larynx is anchored to maximize warmth and stability.

Notice how the jaw and face are optimally placed to keep the larynx in the anchored position.

If we use a car analogy, singing in neutral position is like driving in an upper gear-your voice, and the car, sing easily here, and you can go as high as your range allows you.

SLOPE/THIRD GEAR

Michael McElroy, Broadway Singer, 2009

The slope position has a majority of CT muscle, but adds in about 25% TA muscle. The slope position is used by many jazz singers and classical musical theater performers. It is also used at the top of pop singers ranges, as well as classical male singers who have managed to figure out their break. The vertical position of the larynx is in the easy position in most slope styles, allowing for a warm sound with just a bit of point.

Notice the difference in the facial positions of this classical musical theater singer and the classical singer. Again, this is to optimize laryngeal position.

In our car driving analogy, think of third gear as having more overt power; you can easily drive/ sing along here without too much effort, and you can go pretty high. At the very top, you will probably have to switch to fourth gear.

INCLINE/SECOND GEAR

Billie Holiday, 1947

The incline position has a 50/50 split between CT muscle and TA muscle. The incline position is where most pop and contemporary musical theater singers make their bread and butter. The vertical position of the larynx is in the energized position. The jaw is firm and slightly extended to anchor the larynx in that position. The tongue is ramped and wide, and should touch the upper back molars. The sound quality is piercing and one dimensional, which is why most successful pop singers utilize a mixture of positions in one piece of music, saving the incline position for high, dramatic notes.

Back to our car—think of incline as a really powerful low gear— but it does have some higher pitch limits. You will have to switch to third, then fourth to access the very top notes.

FULL/FIRST GEAR

Jose Carreras, Opera Singer, 2011

The full position is all TAM function. It is the vocal fold position that cracks in both female and male voices. The full position is utilized by male operatic singers and female singers in their lowest range. The vertical position of the larynx is often anchored, to create warmth and stability. The sound is full and loud. If a singer in full position fails to spectrum back to incline or slope as they approach the high, the note will crack to neutral.

Full position is very clearly first gear; very powerful out of the gate, but you can only rev so high before you are in trouble.

PART 4

Now we know the vertical positions of the larynx and the usefulness of that gross motor function. We also know the four fine motor vocal fold positions: neutral, slope, incline and full. The key to mastering these positions is, of course, practice. To my mind, nothing solidifies these positions better than an exercise called spectrum. Spectrum allows the singer to quickly find each position so they can explore the sound possibilities, strengthen different muscle groups, and most importantly, teach the TAMs and the CTMs how to work together. Many of you will find that you are only used to using one muscle group or the other, and have never experienced using them together. It takes coordination, and it takes practice.

Spectrum the voice, going from neutral to incline. Start in neutral around E4. Your vowel sound should be one that optimizes the lowered, relaxed jaw of neutral, like [A]. Men must begin in falsetto! Slowly pull the larynx up and forward by firming your jaw and starting to change the vowel sound toward [ae]. You should now be in slope. Continue to pull the larynx forward and up by adopting the full belter's bite face (squinty eye, smile, broad, ramped tongue). You are now in incline. The sound should be loud, and perhaps a bit ugly. That's fine! The point is to get your muscles used to working in a new way, and sometimes we have to sing "ugly" to learn. Refer to the pictures of different singers singing in the different positions, and watch yourself in a mirror. Your face should mimic theirs—long low jaw transitioning to slight smile with firm jaw, transitioning to a very firm and slightly protruding jaw. Remember: relaxing your jaw only works for singing in neutral styles. That's why classical voice teachers teach it. You cannot belt with a relaxed jaw.

Once you have the spectrum down, start taking it up by half steps. Many of you will find that you are cracking in between the positions. That is because your TAMs and CTMs are completely unsure of how to work together and are trying to take over for each other abruptly. Patience and practice is key; think of a baby just learning to pick something up between two fingers. They don't have the muscle coordination they need to succeed until they do it again and again; the same is the case for a singer new to these techniques.

When you feel confident about spectrum, it's very important to isolate the different positions and sing there. Spectrum a pitch forward, then stop, either in slope, incline or full. Sing a short, five-note scale up and down in one of the positions. Notice what it feels like, how high you can sing in any one of the positions. Notice the quality of the voice and the vast differences you can make in tone quality by changing the position. Notice the range limitations of each position. Remember: if you crack, you have too much TAM action—spectrum back to incline, slope or neutral.

Congratulations! You now have the key to singing in any style you wish. Check out the chart below to give you some guidelines, remembering that these are just an overall baseline. Most great singers will move in and out of laryngeal and vocal fold spectrums to achieve the sound they want at any given time.

Remember: your support mechanism is the foundation for any style of singing. After your body is properly stacked up, get your larynx in the proper position and you've got half the battle won. Practice the four vocal fold positions until they are smooth, and you feel confident in each one, and moving between each one. Lastly, if it hurts, it is wrong. Nothing in any of these positions should feel strained or painful. Quite the contrary, if you are doing it right, it should feel easy. If something hurts, stop immediately and go back to neutral.

STYLE	**Laryngeal Position**	**Vocal fold spectrum**	**Nasality**	**Brightness**
Classical (female)	4	Neutral	None	Bright/Dark
Classical (male)	4	Full	None	Bright/ Dark
Jazz	3	Slope	None/Some	Neutral
Folk	3	Slope/Neutral	None	Neutral
Classic Musical Theater	3	Slope	None	Bright
Contemporary Musical Theater	2	Incline	None/Some	Bright
R&B	2/3	Slope/Incline	None/Some	Dark
Pop	2	Incline	None/Some	Bright
Screamo/Rock	1	Incline/Full	All/Some	Bright

Warming Up the Eyes and Ears

by J.D. Fizzell

Attention Getters

Squash

The director begins by performing a four beat pattern of one kinesthetic gesture. This can be clapping, snapping, patting your head, etc. The singers are instructed to be one movement behind the director (i.e. the director starts, then the singers start four beats thereafter). As the activity goes on, the director should increase the level of difficulty by increasing the tempo, adding concurrent sounds like buzzing, sirens, animal noises, etc. Toward the end of the exercise, incorporate low, full breaths to provide a quick and seamless transition into breathing and phonation warm-ups.

Key to success: Start slowly and simply, like clapping quarter notes.

Dance Jam

This is for the groggy, low energy Monday or the reward on Friday of a great week of rehearsing. The director plays an up-tempo song over speakers and begins leading a dance. The singers are instructed to mirror the director. Then, at some point, the director leaves the front and gets a volunteer to lead the dancing. When a singer is out of ideas or energy, she can leave the front and another singer must quickly take her place. I usually set a countdown rule wherein if someone doesn't replace the leader within five seconds, the game ends.

Key to success: Make sure the song is appropriate and be ready to quickly transition to avoid lack of focus.

Breathing

In For Four

Have the singers place their hands at the bottom of their ribs, touching the thumbs to the ribs and the rest of the fingers on the stomach. Starting with a low, full diaphragmatic breath, inhale and gradually open up your hands. Exhale, pulling hands back towards the body. Then, say "in for four" and breathe in for four beats. Then say "Out for four" and exhale with the singers. Repeat this process in time without breaks, changing to "out for eight, out for twelve," etc. I usually go up to sixteen or twenty. For variety, you can exhale on a hiss.

Key to success: Model well with your own breathing and keep a steady, moderate tempo.

Big "O" Breath

Again, with the hands resting below the bottom of the rib cage, expand them outwards while breathing in on an "O" vowel. Exhale. Start with a whole note value for both the inhalation and exhalation. Then move to a half note, followed by quarter notes, and then eighth notes. Singers will recognize the pattern without you having to say anything. To make the exercise more advanced, sing a note instead of just exhaling. The easiest versions would use a voiced consonant like "n", "m" or "l", followed by an open vowel like "e" or "ah." More difficult versions would use a fricative or aspirate like "free" or "hah".

Key to success: Focus on the onset, the point at which inhalation ends and phonation begins. Be sure that extra air is not being lost here.

PHONATION

The Easy Open

This warm-up is great place to start. It has a three note range, improves unison tuning, and develops proper vowel placement. I choose different vowels on different days based on the literature I'm teaching. Often, I'll start with a closed hum. In addition, I will have students put a cup shaped hand on the side of their face to emulate resonating space.

Keys to success: Start at a B, C, or C sharp and don't go up past an initial note of A or A sharp.

The Placement Helper

I often find that as I teach private voice lessons, brighter vowels like "ee" are much easier for singers to place in a forward position with a raised soft palate. By combining a bright vowel with a closed mouth shape, the focus turns to the onset of the vowel each time. The goal of thie exercise is to transfer the placement of the brighter vowel to the darker one.

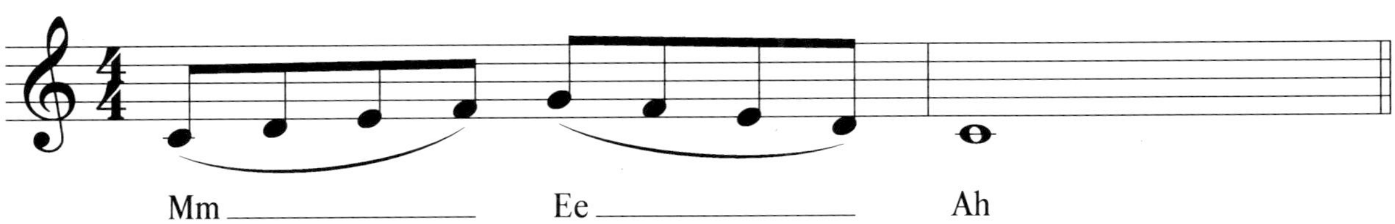

Key to success: Again, keep the key moderate- start at C sharp and end on F or G.

Get It Forward

To help brighten a singer's tone, try this warm-up.

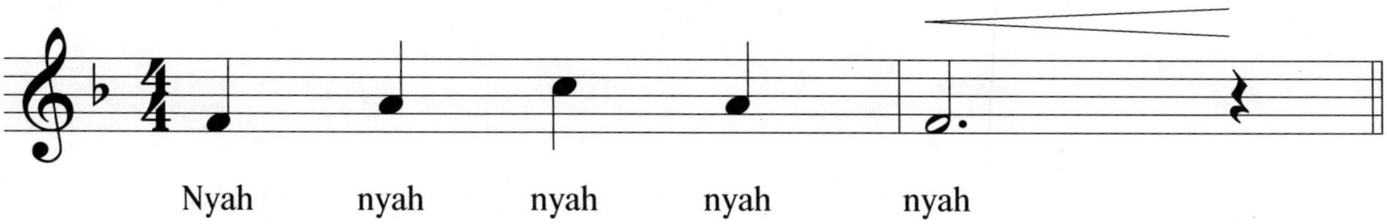

Key to success: Use the "ny" to connect one note to the next, so it is smooth and legato. Remember to keep your vowel tall and vertical on "ah", not spread and horizontal.

Articulation

The Hot Stove

This is one of the best warm-ups out there in my opinion, because it does so much at once. I first saw it in rehearsal with my choral mentor, Dr. Jeff Johnson at The University of Kentucky. Start by placing one hand palm up in front of you and start to lightly tap it with a finger of your other hand. Say, "Hot stove!" as you show the lightness and quickness with which you pull your finger away from your hand. Then you alternate to tapping the other hand, switching back and forth each time. Then sing this pattern:

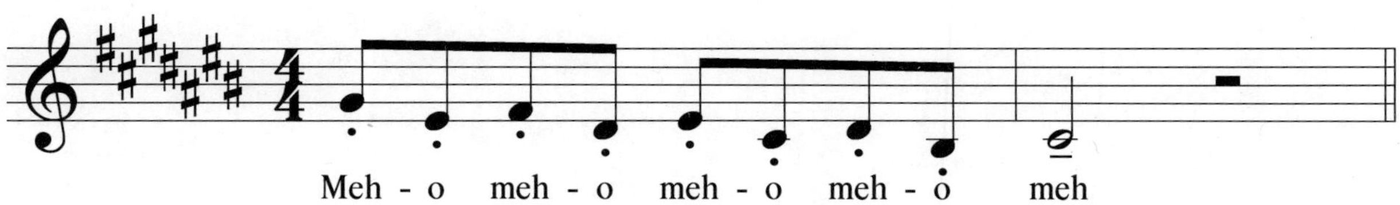

You can then change the articulation to legato by making your hands flat and change your alternation of hands to a smooth one. You can even alter the tempo and dynamics by going faster or slower and increasing or decreasing the size of your gesture. You can also add accents by using a big gesture on one beat followed by small gestures immediately after.

Key to success: Keep a moderate tempo and don't get too big with your gesture size.

Dynamics

One to Eight

Place your hands together like a clap, directly in front of you. Build a chord, then start singing *1-2-3-4-5-6-7-8* as you expand your hands outward. Start at pianissimo at 1 and build to fortissimo at 8, then reverse the process.

You can vary this warm-up in a variety of ways:

- Change the number of beats to 4, 2, 6, 10, etc.
- Use different dynamics at the beginning and end of the exercise
- Sing on vowels instead of numbers and audiate the counting
- Choose a word from a piece you are doing and create the dynamic contrast you want in that phrasing

Key to success: Make the singers perform the kinesthetic gesture, too.

Range Extension

The Lip or Tongue Trill

Slide up a perfect 5th and back down on a lip trill or (more advanced) tongue trill. Another benefit of this exercise is that it is not easy to do without substantial breath support. I'll often reinforce that support by having singers use the rib hand open and close from the "In For Four" warm-up. This is also great for very quickly warming up your voice.

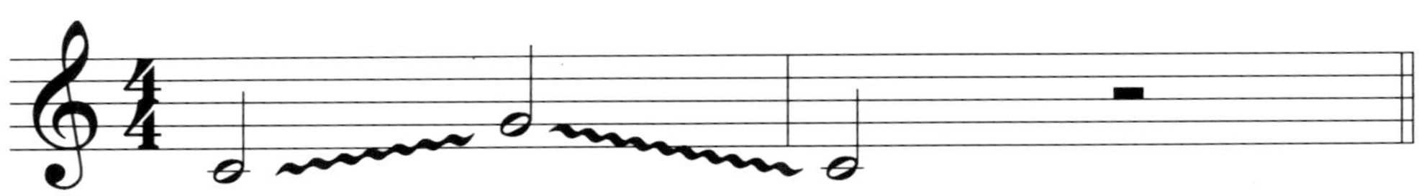

Key to success: Start in the middle of the range, B or C.

Zee Yah

This extends the range without letting singers push their voices.

Key to success: When modeling the exercise, be sure to keep a light tone.

Build a Chord, Any Chord

Build a major chord that works for your particular voicing. Sing the chord on any open vowel. I usually begin with a closed vowel like "oo" so singers can hear better. Instruct them to hold the chord, stagger breathing when necessary, and then point up and have them all go up a half step. Once that has tuned, go back down a half step. Then go down a half step and back up to the original chord. As your singers get better at this, isolate individual sections and move them up or down by half step.

Key to success: Plan where you are going in advance to ensure success (i.e. don't end on a "weird" chord that doesn't sound "right").

Half Step Over Counts

Point your two index fingers horizontally in front of you at each other. Sing a G on "loo." Then raise one hand up higher, maintaining a horizontal plane for your index finger, and sing a G sharp. Then go back down to G and even fingers. Have the singers repeat this process. Then, quickly slide your finger up and back down, sliding the note you sing from G to G sharp. Then go back down. Have singers repeat, also using their fingers. As they get better at tuning, increase the difficulty by sliding through the half step over 2 beats, then 4 beats, then 6 beats, then 8 beats.

Keys to success: Don't move on to a higher number of beats before singers have succeeded with the previous level.

Section II: The Warm-ups

by Deke Sharon

POP

Three-Part Guitar Texture Warm-up

Guitar textures are common in contemporary a cappella, requiring multiple parts to sing the strummed strings as a unit. In addition to complex rhythms, the syllables are often unexpected, as in this warm-up: "zh" should be sung like the sound you make when you say "did you", which sounds a little like it should be spelled "didzhoo."

Skills: Syllables, Rhythm

zhing a ning a nung a ning a zhing zhing a zhing a ning a nung a ning a zhing zhing a
zhing a ning a nung a ning a zhing zhing a zhing a ning a nung a ning a zhing zhing a
zhing a ning a nung a ning a zhing zhing a zhing a ning a nung a ning a zhing zhing a
zhing a ning a nung a ning a zhing zhing a
zhing a ning a nung a ning a zhing zhing a
zhing a ning a nung a ning a zhing zhing a
zhung a nung a nung a nung a nung a
zhung a nung a nung a nung a nung a
zha
nung a nung a nung a nung nung
nung a nung a nung a nung nung

Three-Part Stacked Arpeggiation Warm-up

Usually arpeggiations are built one note at a time but occasionally they are "stacked" with multiple notes happening at once, as happens in Schubert's "Ave Maria." When this happens, it's even more important to have tone be consistent between parts, as well as any register shifting not resulting in a difference in timbre or volume within or between the parts. The syllable written is "thm" (pizzicato strings) but can be easily changed to other syllables to practice consistency across a variety of vowels.

Skills: Tone, Syllables, Rhythm, Intervals

Three-Part Tone Matching Warm-up

Taken from my song "After You" (from The House Jacks' album "Unbroken"), this warm-up is in two parts. The first is a pattern that requires a register shift for most sopranos while maintaining a very uniform tone, one that's echoed by the altos (who also must maintain a consistent tone). The second section involves leaps. All the while, the focus should be on maintaining a clear, consistent tone (as well pitch and rhythm, of course).

Skills: Tone, Intervals, Rhythm

Loh loh loh loh loh loh loh loh
Loh loh loh loh loh loh loh loh
9
Loh loh
loh loh loh loh loh loh loh loh loh loh loh loh
loh loh loh loh loh loh loh loh loh loh loh loh
11
loh loh loh
loh loh loh loh loh loh loh loh loh loh loh loh
loh loh loh loh loh loh loh loh loh loh loh loh
14
loh loh loh

Arpeggiation warm-up

Arpeggiations are found throughout many styles of a cappella (remember "Mr. Sandman/Mr. Santa"?) so it's important to learn how to strike a note cleanly in perfect tune and rhythm while matching the same vowel and dynamic level as the rest of your group so that you sound like one unified instrument. This exercise can be done by the entire group or by one on a part, and you can change the individuals which, ideally, will not result in a significant difference in tone/timbre. Once this becomes easy, change the syllables and speed it up to increase the challenge.

Skills: Rhythm, Tone, Dynamics

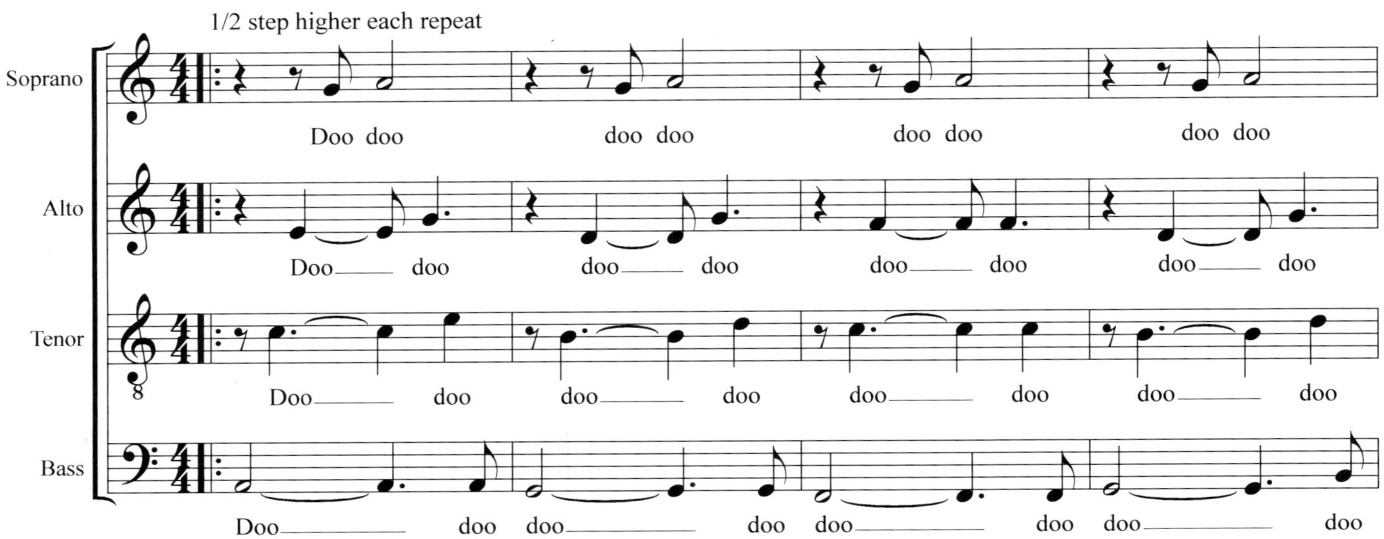

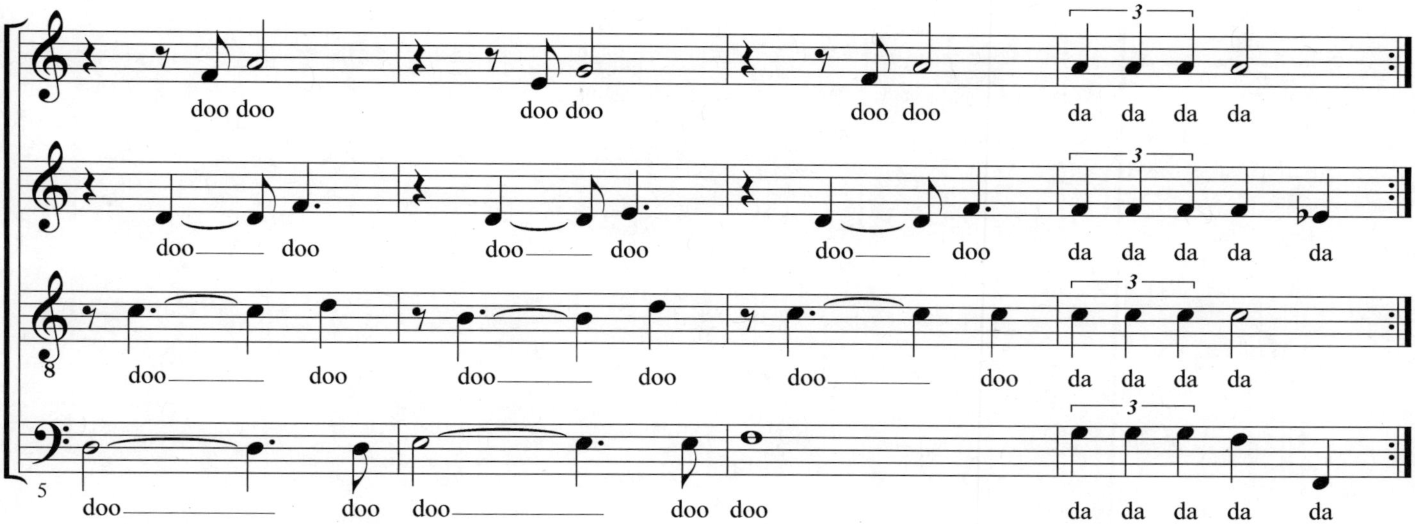

(First measure after repeat will be:)

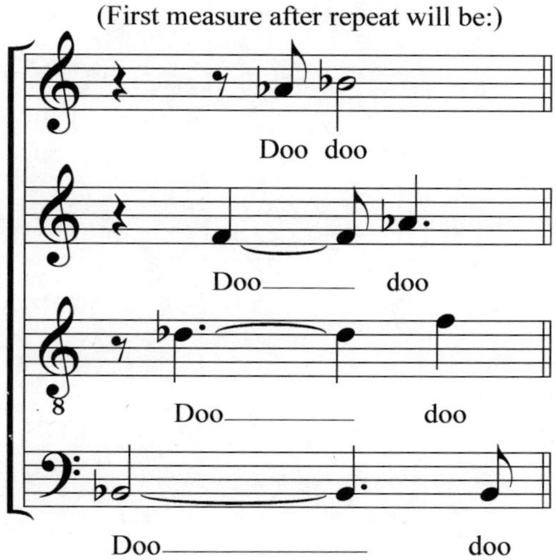

cascade warm-up

This is a modified version of a warm-up I learned back when I was a member of the Tufts Beelzebubs. The sopranos hold a pitch and the rest of the parts cascade downward, eventually resolving the chord, at which point the director can indicate if the next cascade should be down or up a half step. (It's also possible to move several half steps before starting the next cascade.)

Skills: Intonation, Blend, Balance

CHOOSE YOUR OWN SYLLABLES WARM-UP (EVERYWHERE I GO)

Many people approach music as though it's something created entirely by others and it's their job to merely reproduce perfect decisions, but the history of music doesn't work that way. This exercise engages your singers' creativity by having them choose their own background syllables for a pop song that they've never heard before (written by me and my kids). Start with the chorus: learn the parts, and have the basses decide on a syllable that best suits them. Then go back to the top of the song and figure out a suitable syllable for the upper parts, and perhaps change the bass syllable there as well. Once that's sounding good you can replace the existing lyrics with scat syllables of your own choosing.

Skills: Syllables, Improvisation

and fly - ing so - lo Once up - on a time I did - n't know
dy - nam - ic du - o al - ways on my mind a tea for two
why I was sad and feel - ing so low but then
and you for me and me for you o my love
you came a - long and made my life a beau - ti - ful song
for you's so strong I'll be with you my whole life long

Chorus
made my life a beau-ti-ful song
be with you my whole life long
Go go I
Ev-'ry-where I go you're right be-side
made my life a beau-ti-ful song
be with you my whole life long
Go go I
go go I go go and
me ev-'ry-where I go you're in my heart
go go I go go and
ev-'ry-where and ev-'ry-where I go go I
Ev-'ry-where I go ev-'ry-where I
ev-'ry-where and ev-'ry-where I go go I

go go I go go and ev - 'ry - where and ev - 'ry - where I
go ev - 'ry - where I go
go go I go go and ev - 'ry - where and ev - 'ry - where I
22

Dense Texture Warm-up

Sometimes the lightest, gentlest textures in a cappella songs are deceptive, in that they're the result of many complex parts, like tiny, carefully interwoven silk threads. Each part needs to be perfectly balanced and in tune for this particular vocal fabric to shimmer. Start rehearsing this at a slow tempo and gradually accelerate once you have all of the pieces properly interlocked, with the Soprano II melody only slightly louder than the other parts (should be discernable even when it's lower in pitch than the soprano).

Skills: Blend, Balance, Improvisation.

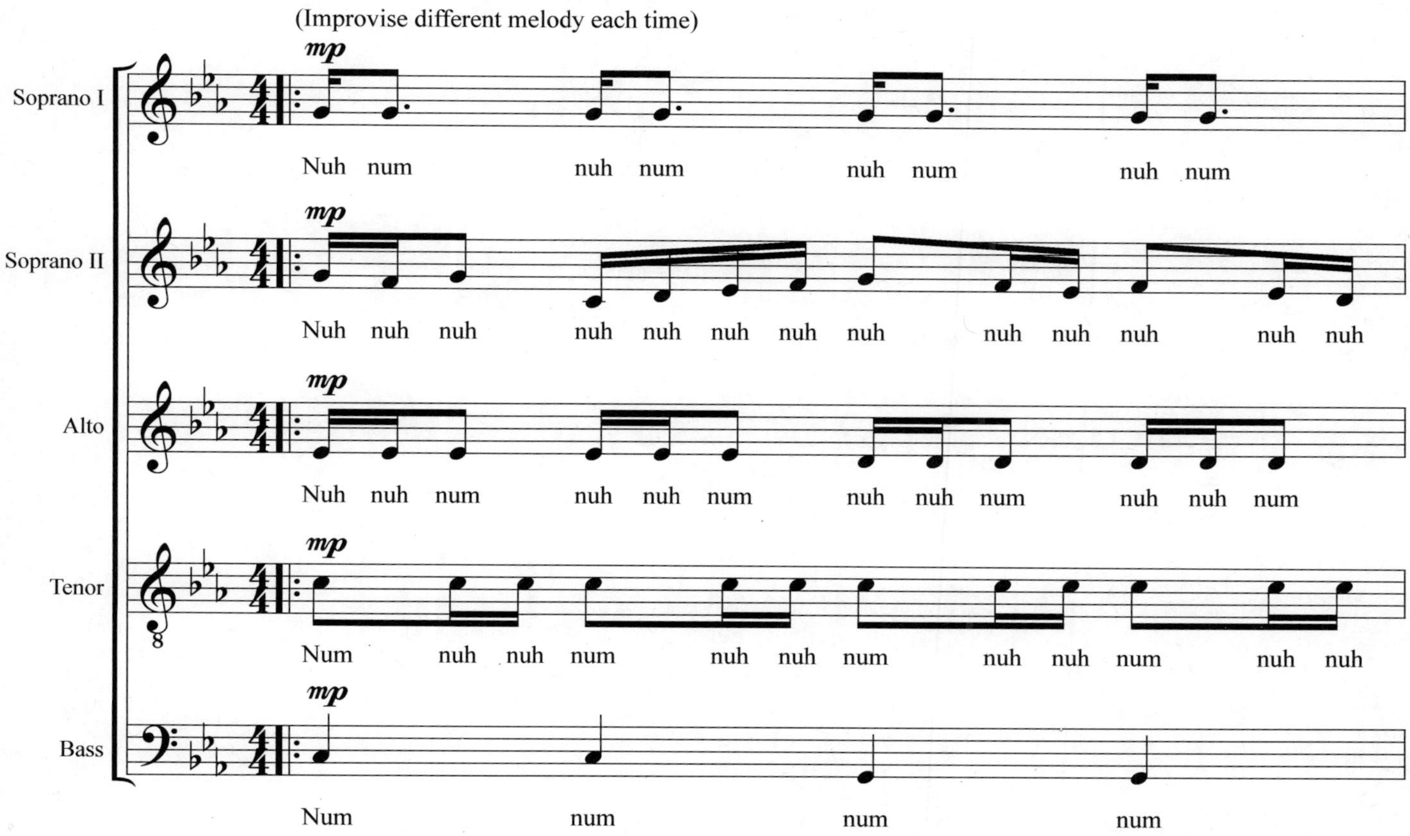

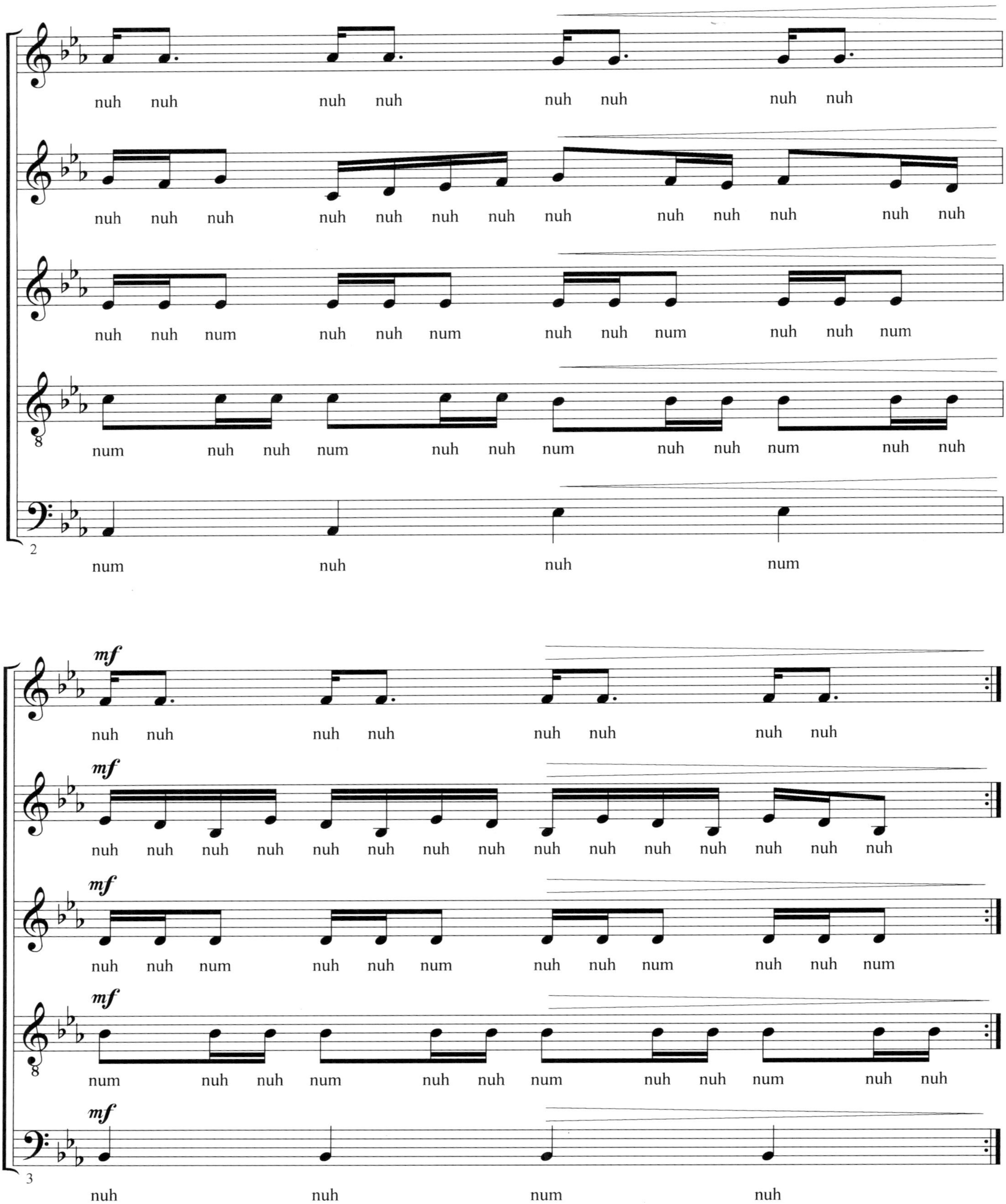
nuh nuh nuh nuh nuh nuh nuh nuh
nuh nuh nuh nuh nuh nuh nuh nuh nuh nuh nuh nuh nuh nuh
nuh nuh num nuh nuh num nuh nuh num nuh nuh num
num nuh nuh num nuh nuh num nuh nuh num nuh nuh
2
num nuh nuh num
mf
nuh nuh nuh nuh nuh nuh nuh nuh
mf
nuh nuh nuh nuh nuh nuh nuh nuh nuh nuh nuh nuh nuh nuh nuh
mf
nuh nuh num nuh nuh num nuh nuh num nuh nuh num
mf
num nuh nuh num nuh nuh num nuh nuh num nuh nuh
mf
3
nuh nuh num nuh

DIT DIT Warm-up

This warm-up is designed to help beginning groups listen and lock a straightforward modern a cappella texture. Once you have this mastered, you can raise or lower the pattern with each repeat: make the group watch you and signal by pointing up or down during the last beat (or two beats if you're feeling generous), which will get them used to watching you closely, as well as retuning a pattern in different keys (a valuable skill when you decide to take an entire song up or down a whole step, especially for those who have perfect pitch or specific pitch memory, both of which can be a burden at times).

Skills: Rhythm, Pitch

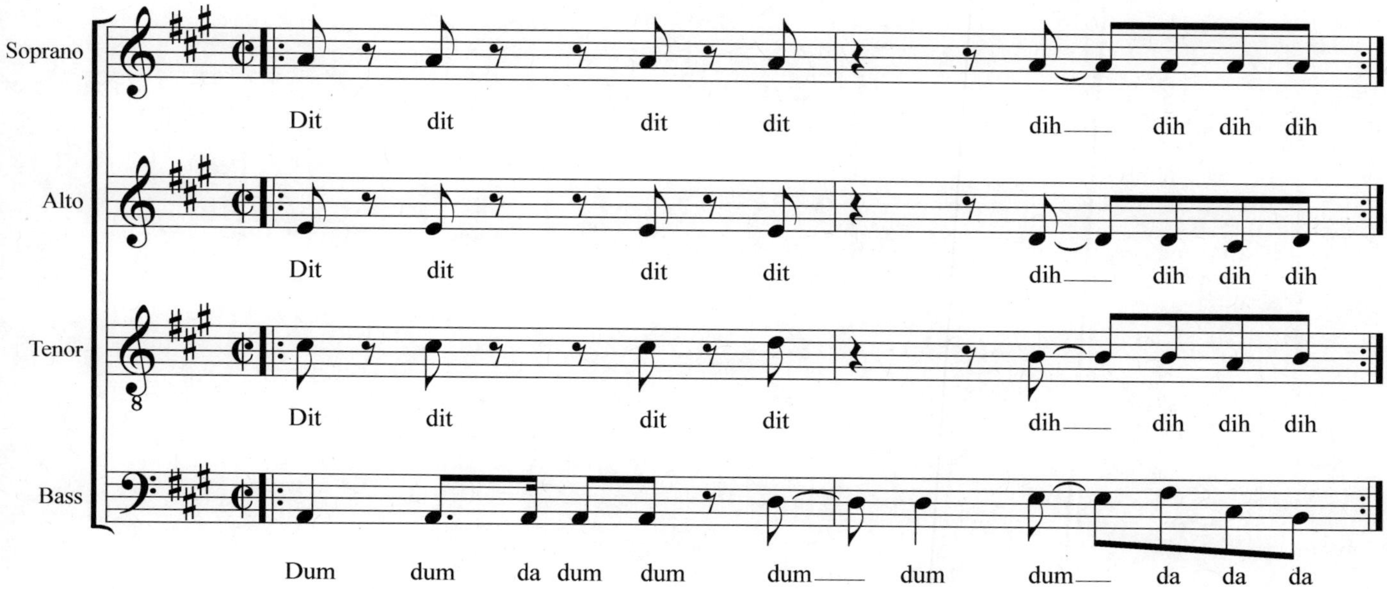

DOO-WOP WARM-UP

Sometimes warm-ups should just be fun, and this one is. Repeat as many times as you'd like, with different people on the solo line, improvising their own doo wop style melody (falsetto is not only allowed, it's encouraged). Background syllables can also be changed—the more ridiculous the better.

Skills: Blend, Balance, Improvisation, Tone, Syllables, Solo

2
rit.
na na na na na na na oo wee oo
la oo wee oo doo
la oo wee oo doo doo
la oo wee oo doo doo doo
5
dip bow bow bow oo

DYNAMICS WARM-UP (HOUSE OF THE RISING SUN)

Sadly, most young musicians aren't exposed to true dynamics in music on a daily basis, since pretty much everything nowadays is compressed to the point of being one consistent volume throughout. For this reason, even experienced singers can be reluctant to sing in the true extremes of their range, from whisper-soft to rattling-loud. This passage is designed to give you an opportunity to start from where the singers can barely produce tone swelling to where their voices are almost at a yell, then quickly decrescendo back. If your singers are struggling to find the full range of dynamics, try using a "noo" syllable for soft, "no" for medium, and "nah" for loud.

Skills: Dynamics

mp
no no no no no no no no no no no no no no no no no no
mp
no no no no no no no no no no no no no no no no no no
mp
no no no no no no no no no no no no no no no no no no
mp
7
done not to spend their
mf
f
no no no no no no no no no no no no! no no no no no no
mf
f
no no no no no no no no no no no no! no no no no no no
mf
f
no no no no no no no no no no no no! no no no no no no
mf
f
10
lives in mis - er - y mis - er - y in the
ff
p
no no no no no no no no no no no no no no no no no no no!
ff
p
no no no no no no no no no no no no no no no no no no no!
ff
p
no no no no no no no no no no no no no no no no no no no!
ff
p
13
house of the ris - ing sun no!

Dynamic & Syllable Shift Warm-up

Often in contemporary a cappella, particularly if there are a limited number of vocal parts (as happens live, in the studio you can overdub endlessly), you'll find the background texture and syllables shifting, as if you're shifting from one instrument to another. In this warm-up, the "bap" represents a horn section, with the "doot" more of a keyboard. As those syllables shift, so should the dynamics, the horns being louder than the keyboard (in fact, in a recording, a keyboard part would likely be playing the entire time, just covered up by the much louder horns). The bass, however, shouldn't change dynamic level throughout.

Skills: Dynamics, Syllables, Balance

bap bap ba ba da ba da bap bap
bap bap ba ba da ba da bap bap
bap bap ba ba da ba da bap bap
5
da ba da ba da ba ba da ba
mp
f
doot doo doot doo be doo be doo ba ba da da ba dap bap
doot doo doot doo be doo be doo ba ba da da ba dap bap
doot doo doot doo be doo be doo ba ba da da ba dap bap
7
da ba ba da ba da ba da ba da ba da ba da ba da ba
doo doot doo doot doo doot doo be doo be doo ba yeah!
doot doo doot doo be doo be doo ba yeah!
doot doo doot doo be doo be doo ba yeah!
10
dap bap da ba ba da ba da ba ba da ba yeah!

Group Melodic Phrasing (SFO) Warm-up

In a cappella as well as in several styles of popular music, sometimes a tune isn't just one line, it's a combination of multiple parallel melodic lines, all tightly phrased together. Where should everyone swoop up together? Fall off? Sing straight tone as opposed to kick into vibrato? Play with this little jingle written for and sung at the opening of San Francisco Airport Terminal Two. Suggestion: Have individuals sing the line along in their own style, then have the group copy their exact phrasing (an effective method for any melody sung by a group).

Skills: Blend, Balance, Tone, Phrasing

Half Step (Pudding) Warm-up

This relatively straightforward warm-up is an opportunity to lock down moving by half steps in context. This odd little piece of music was written for a documentary movie that was never released, in which certain statements by political figures would then be animated, underscored with little ditties. You can hear this, and others from the same movie, on the House Jacks album "BlackJack."

Skills: Pitch, Intervals

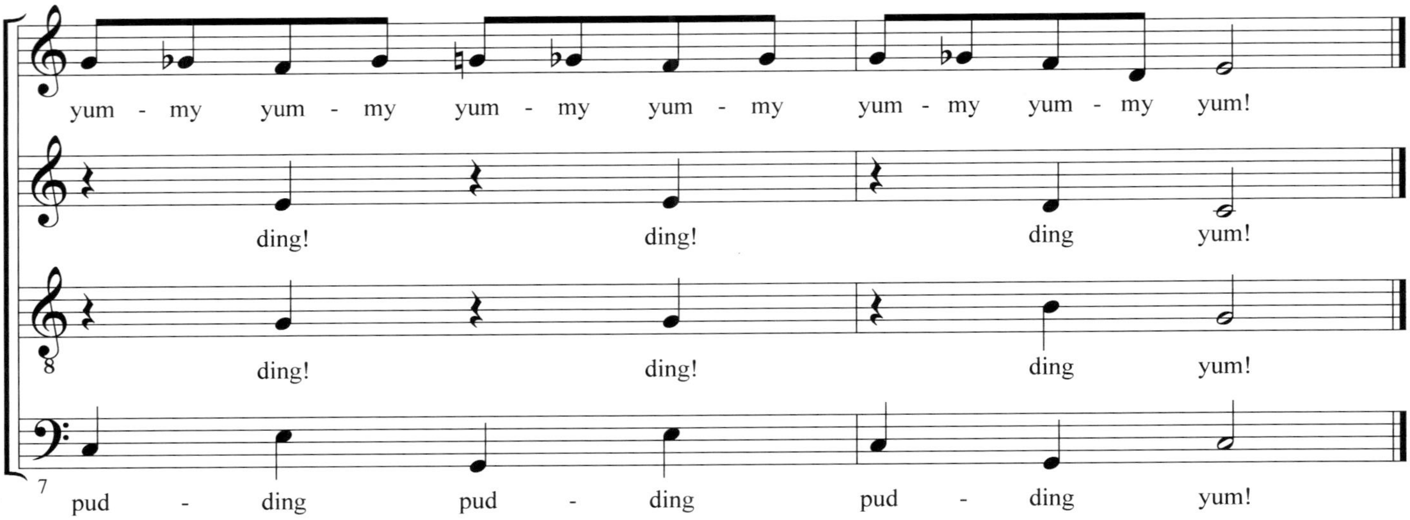

Held Note Against Pattern Warm-up

It would seem that holding a note would be the easiest thing you can do in a cappella, but in fact there are times it can be a challenge. In this warm-up there will be two opposing forces: the desire to bend the note up as the other parts all ascend, and the note slowing bending down as focus is lost and the note drifts flat because it's not properly supported (worst case: this happens at the same time by different members of the same vocal part). Once this is mastered at pitch, move it up or down a half step each time, resetting the pitch center.

Skills: Intonation, Balance, Pitch

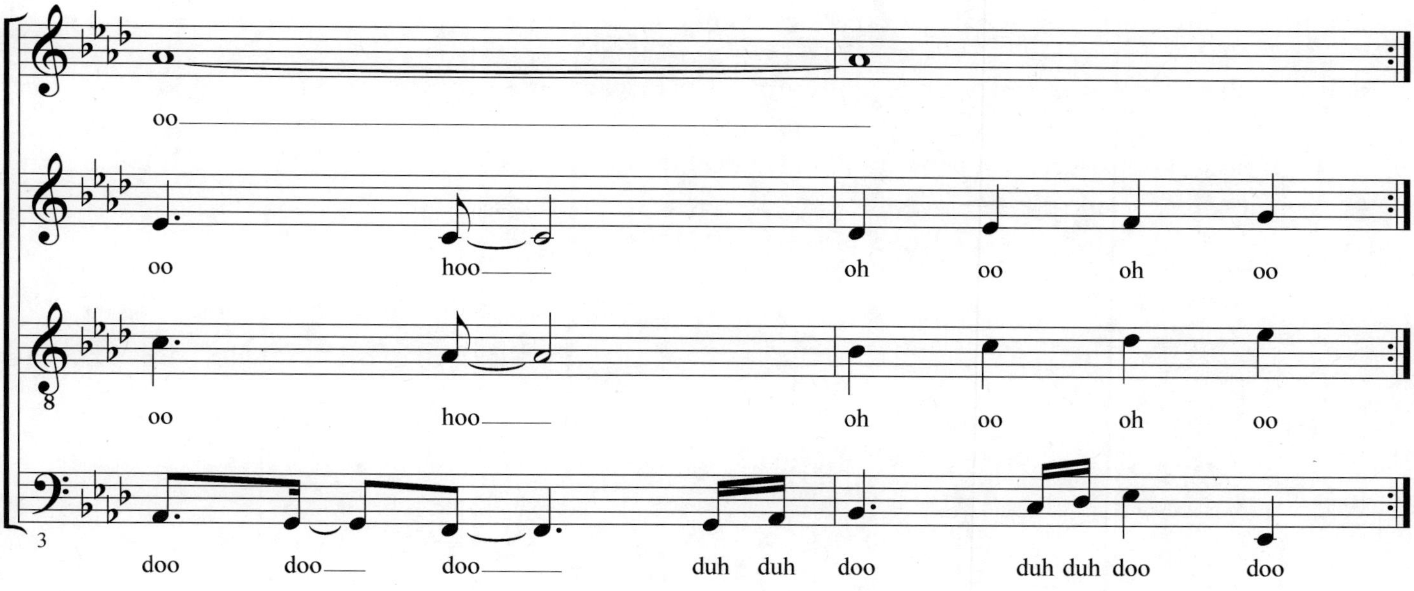
oo
oo hoo oh oo oh oo
oo hoo oh oo oh oo
3
doo doo doo duh duh doo duh duh doo doo

Increasing Texture Warm-Up (Man of Constant Sorrow)

Rather than just focus on a single texture, this warm-up includes an entire arrangement of "Man of Constant Sorrow" (from the Coen Brothers movie "O Brother, Where Art Thou?"). The arrangement starts simple and slowly grows as the song grows in intensity. Pay attention to maintaining balance and a consistent texture as the rhythms grow more complex. Feel free to use just a section as a warm-up, or sing the entire song.

Skills: Rhythm, Pitch, Dynamics, Balance

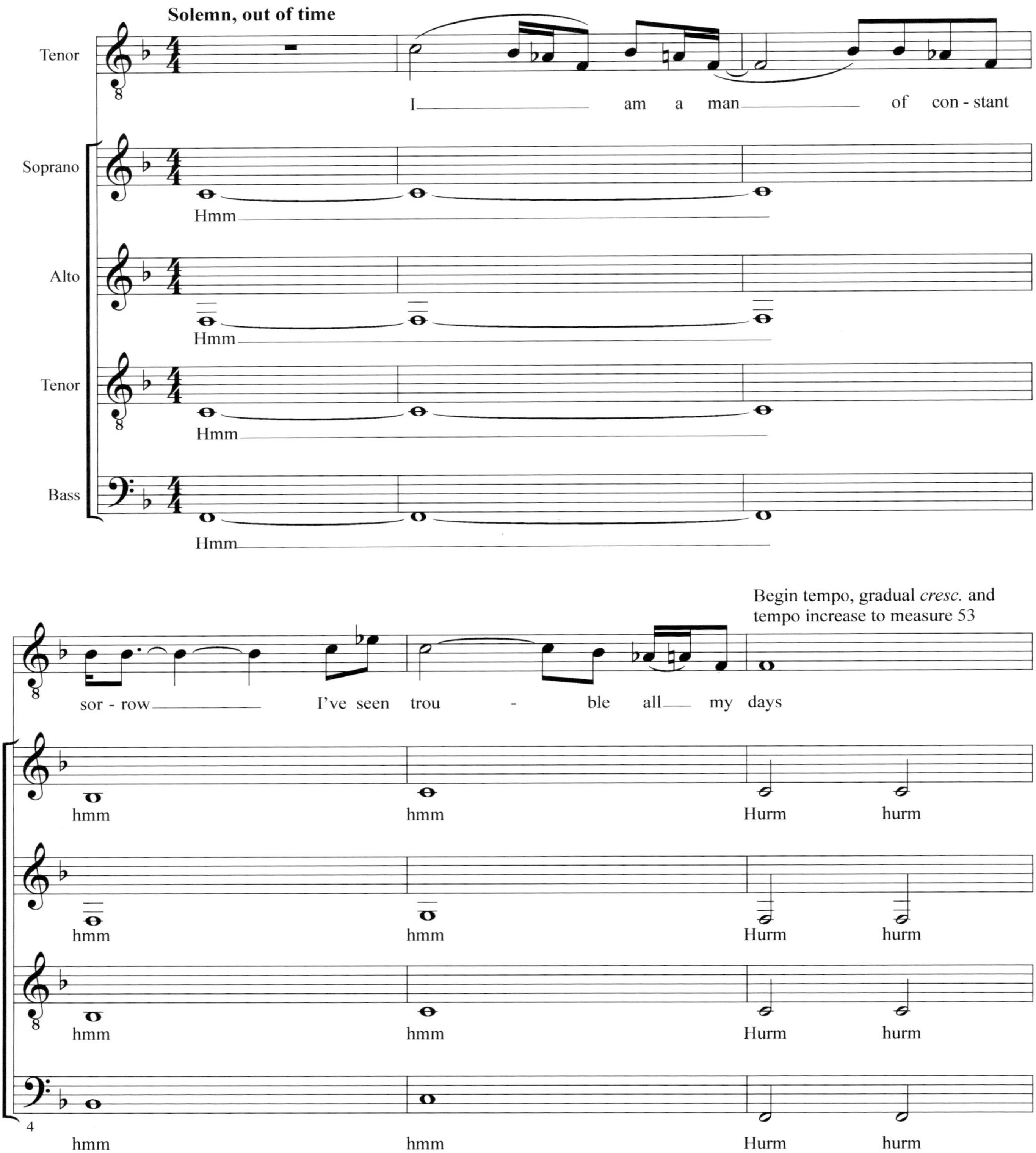

I bid fare - well to ol' Ken- tuc - ky the place where
hurm hurm hurm hurm hurm hurm
hurm hurm hurm hurm hurm hurm
hurm hurm hurm hurm hurm hurm
7
hurm hurm hurm hurm hurm hurm
I was born and raised.
hurm hurm hurm The place where he was born and
hurm hurm hurm The place where he was born and
hurm hurm hurm The place where he was born and
10
hurm hurm hurm hurm hurm hurm

Optional: change soloists each verse
For six long years
raised. Dung dung dung dung dung dung dung dung
raised. Duh nung dung dung dung dung dung dung
raised. Dung dung dung
Dung dung dung dung dung dung dung dung
13
I've been in trou - ble, no pleas - ure
dung dung dung dung dung dung dung dung
dung dung dung dung dung dung dung dung
dung dung dung dung
dung dung dung dung dung dung dung dung
15

on earth I've found
dung dung dung dung dung dung dung
dung dung dung dung dung dung dung dung
dung dung dung duh nuh dung dung duh nung duh
17
dung dung dung dung dung dung dung dung
For in this world, I'm bound to
dung dung dung dung dung dung dung
dung dung dung dung dung dung dung dung
nung duh nung duh nung dung duh nuh dung dung duhdung dung duh nung duh
19
dung dung dung dung dung dung dung dung

ram - ble, I have no friends to help me
dung dung dung dung dung dung dung dung
dung dung dung dung dung dung dung dung
nung duh nung duh nung dung duh nuh dung dung duh dung nung dung duh nuh
21
dung dung dung dung dung dung dung dung
now.
dung dung dung He has no friends to help him
dung dung He has no friends to help him
dung dung duh dung He has no friends to help him
23
dung dung tung tuh nuh tung tuh nuh tung tuh nuh tung tuh nuh tung tuh nuh tung tuh nuh

It's fair thee well,
now. Tung tuh nuh tung tung tuh nuh tung tung tuh nuh tung tung tuh nuh
now. Tuh nuh tung tung tuh nuh tung tung tuh nuh tung tung tuh nuh tung
now. Tung tung tung tung tung tung tung
tung tuh nuh tung tuh nuh tung tuh nuh tung tuh nuh tung tuh nuh tung tuh nuh tung tuh nuh tung tuh nuh
25
my old true lov - er, I nev-er ex -
now tung tuh nuh tung tung tuh nuh tung tung tuh nuh tung tung tuh nuh
now tuh nuh tung tung tuh nuh tung tung tuh nuh tung tung tuh nuh tung
now tung tung tung tung tung tung tung
tung tuh nuh tung tuh nuh tung tuh nuh tung tuh nuh tung tuh nuh tung tuh nuh tung tuh nuh tung tuh nuh
27

pec - ted to see you a - gain.
now tung tuh nuh tung tung tuh nuh tung tung tuh nuh tung tung tuh nuh
now tuh nuh tung tung tuh nuh tung tung tuh nuh tung tung tuh nuh tung
now tung tung tung tung tung tung tung
29
tung tuh nuh tung tuh nuh tung tuh nuh tung tuh nuh tung tuh nuh tung tuh nuh tung tuh nuh tung tuh nuh
For I'm bound to ride that North-ern
now tung tuh nuh tung tung tuh nuh tung tung tuh nuh tung tung tuh nuh
now tuh nuh tung tung tuh nuh tung tung tuh nuh tung tung tuh nuh tung
now tung tung tung tung tung tung tung
31
tung tuh nuh tung tuh nuh tung tuh nuh tung tuh nuh tung tuh nuh tung tuh nuh tung tuh nuh tung tuh nuh

Rail - road. Per - haps I'll die up - on this
now tung tuh nuh tung tung tuh nuh tung tung tuh nuh tung tung tuh nuh
now tuh nuh tung tung tuh nuh tung tung tuh nuh tung tung tuh nuh tung
now tung tung tung tung tung tung tung
33
tung tuh nuh tung tuh nuh tung tuh nuh tung tuh nuh tung tuh nuh tung tuh nuh tung tuh nuh tung tuh nuh
train.
train Per - haps he'll die up - on this
train Per - haps he'll die up - on this
train Per - haps he'll die up - on this
35
tung tuh nuh tung tuh nuh tung tuh nuh tung tuh nuh Chung ch - kung chung ch - kung

You can bu - ry me
train. Ch kh chung ch kh chung ch kh chung ch kh chung ch kh chung ch kh chung ch kh chung ch kh
train. Kh chung ch kh chung ch kh chung ch kh chung ch kh chung ch kh chung ch kh chung ch kh chung
train. Kung kh ch kung kh ch kung kh ch kung kh ch kung kh ch kung kh ch kung kh ch kung kh
37
chung ch - kung chung ch - kung chung ch - kung chung ch - kung
in Sun - ny Val - ley. For man - y
chung ch kh chung ch kh chung ch kh chung ch kh chung ch kh chung ch kh chung ch kh chung ch kh
ch kh chung ch kh chung ch kh chung ch kh chung ch kh chung ch kh chung ch kh chung ch kh chung
ch kung kh ch kung kh ch kung kh ch kung kh ch kung kh ch kung kh ch kung kh ch kung kh
39
chung ch - kung chung ch - kung chung ch - kung chung ch - kung

years there I may lay.
chung ch kh chung ch kh chung ch kh chung ch kh chung kh chung kh chung kh chung kh
ch kh chung ch kh chung ch kh chung ch kh chung ch chung ch chung ch chung ch chung
ch kung kh ch kung kh ch kung kh ch kung kh ch-kung ch-kung ch-kung ch-kung
41
chung ch-kung chung ch-kung chung ch-kung chung ch-kung
And you will learn to love an -
chung kh chung kh chung kh chung kh chung kh chung kh chung kh chung kh
ch chung ch chung ch chung ch chung ch chung ch chung ch chung ch chung
ch-kung ch-kung ch-kung ch-kung ch-kung ch-kung ch-kung ch-kung
43
chung ch-kung chung ch-kung chung ch-kung chung ch-kung

45
oth - er while I am sleep - ing in my
chung kh chung kh chung kh chung kh chung kh chung kh chung kh chung kh
ch chung ch chung ch chung ch chung ch chung ch chung ch chung ch chung
ch-kung ch-kung ch-kung ch-kung ch-kung ch-kung ch-kung ch-kung
chung ch-kung chung ch-kung chung ch-kung chung ch-kung
47
grave.
Hmm While he is sleep - ing in his
Hmm While he is sleep - ing in his
Hmm While he is sleep - ing in his
chung ch - kung chung ch - kung Jung jih kuh jung jih kuh jung jih kuh jung jih kuh

May - be your friends -
grave. Jih kuh jih kuh jih kuh jih kuh jih kuh jih kuh jih kuh jung jih kuh jih kuh jih kuh jih kuh jih kuh jih kuh jih kuh
grave. Jih kuh jih kuh jih kuh jih kuh jih kuh jih kuh jih kuh jung jih kuh jih kuh jih kuh jih kuh jih kuh jih kuh jih kuh
grave. Jih kuh jih kuh jih kuh jih kuh jih kuh jih kuh jih kuh jung jih kuh jih kuh jih kuh jih kuh jih kuh jih kuh jih kuh
49
jung jih kuh jung jih kuh jung jih kuh jung jih kuh jung jih kuh jung jih kuh jung jih kuh jung jih kuh
think I'm just a stran - ger. My face you
jung jih kuh jih kuh jih kuh jih kuh jih kuh jih kuh jih kuh jung jih kuh jih kuh jih kuh jih kuh jih kuh jih kuh jih kuh
jung jih kuh jih kuh jih kuh jih kuh jih kuh jih kuh jih kuh jung jih kuh jih kuh jih kuh jih kuh jih kuh jih kuh jih kuh
jung jih kuh jih kuh jih kuh jih kuh jih kuh jih kuh jih kuh jung jih kuh jih kuh jih kuh jih kuh jih kuh jih kuh jih kuh
51
jung jih kuh jung jih kuh jung jih kuh jung jih kuh jung jih kuh jung jih kuh jung jih kuh jung jih kuh

Out of time, ala beginning:
decresc.
nev - er will see no more.
jung jih kuh jih kuh jih kuh jih kuh jih kuh jih kuh jih kuh more
jung jih kuh jih kuh jih kuh jih kuh jih kuh jih kuh jih kuh more
jung jih kuh jih kuh jih kuh jih kuh jih kuh jih kuh jih kuh more
53
jung jih kuh jung jih kuh jung jih kuh jung jih kuh more
But there is one prom - ise that is giv - en, I'll see you
Hmm hmm
Hmm hmm
Hmm hmm
55
Hmm hmm

on God's gold - en shore.
hmm hmm He'll meet you on God's gold - en shore.
hmm hmm He'll meet you on God's gold - en shore.
hmm hmm He'll meet you on God's gold - en shore.
58
hmm hmm God's gold - en shore.

Leaping Chromatics Warm-up (Adventure Day)

Stevie Wonder is a constant inspiration for many reasons, one of which is his ability to build catchy pop songs atop increasingly complex and unexpected chord progressions. This song ("Adventure Day," on The House Jacks album "Unbroken") weaves together leaps and chromatics, two more complex musical elements essential for all a cappella singers to master.

Skills: Intervals, Pitch, Intonation

dant dit dit dit dant dit dit dit dit
ven - ture day e ay e ay e ay e
ven - ture day e ay e ay e ay e
duh d duh duh duh duh duh d duh duh duh duh
5
na na na na na na na na na na na na
ay na na na na na na na na na na na na
ay na na na na na na na na na na na na
duh d duh duh duh duh duh d duh duh duh duh
7
1
2
Come with me (nah)
duh d duh duh duh duh dum
9

Lyrics vs Backgrounds Warm-up (Great Big U.S.A.)

A cappella groups create all of the sound, from the melody, to vocal harmonies, to the rhythm section and other instruments. Balancing these elements can be challenging, especially when a section rapidly jumps back and forth between melodic and background parts. This song, found on The House Jacks album "Get Down Mr. President," will give your singers an opportunity to practice modulating their own volume levels as they move to and from lyrics.

Skills: Balance, Dynamics

drive your car all day sha la oo sha la
drive your car all day sha la oo sha la
all day and ev - 'ry - thing will be
5
doh doh doh doh doh doh doh doh doh doh doh doh
oo sha la oo in the Great Big U S A
oo sha la oo in the Great Big U S A
O K in the Great Big U S A
7
doh doh doh doh doh doh Great Big U S

Pass the Chord Warm-Up

I designed this warm-up to focus on giving individuals an opportunity to focus on blending with others when in a variety of different configurations. This can work with any number of individuals, and the chord can be expanded to 4 or 5 chord factors (get as dense and dissonant as you'd like with any vowel of your choosing, once your singers understand the process) but for this example I'll start with a simple triad and seven singers, so you can see how it gets passed around, with every singer eventually singing every note (falsetto is fine – the key is to focus on balancing and blending regardless where someone is in their range/tessitura), ending where you began. Have everyone start in a circle, give the starting pitches to three singers, and snap the four count consistently, with the singers who are singing notes stepping in toward the center of the circle, and stepping back out once they stop singing. As a result you'll have people moving toward and away from the center slowly throughout the exercise.

Skills: Balance, Blend, Tone

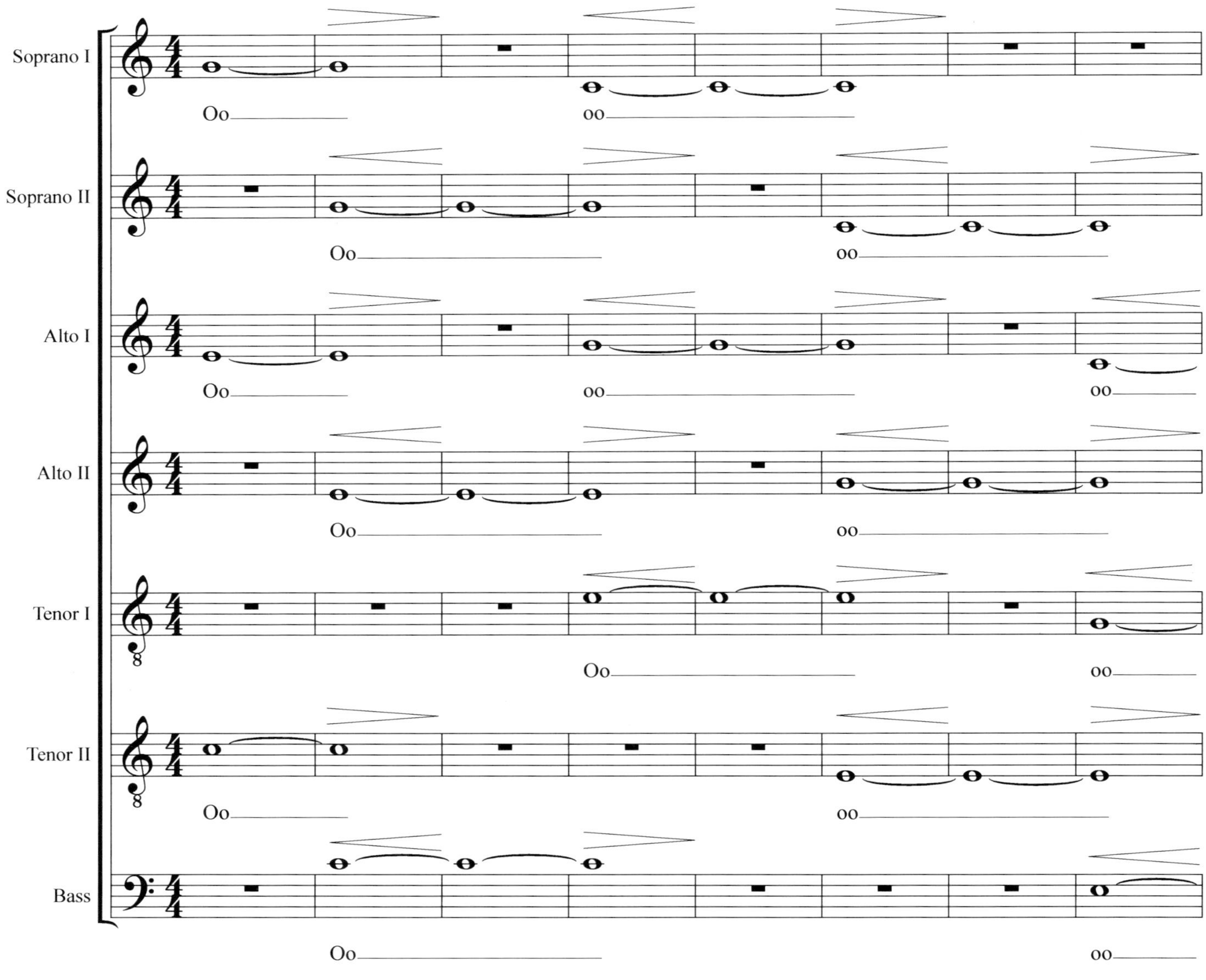

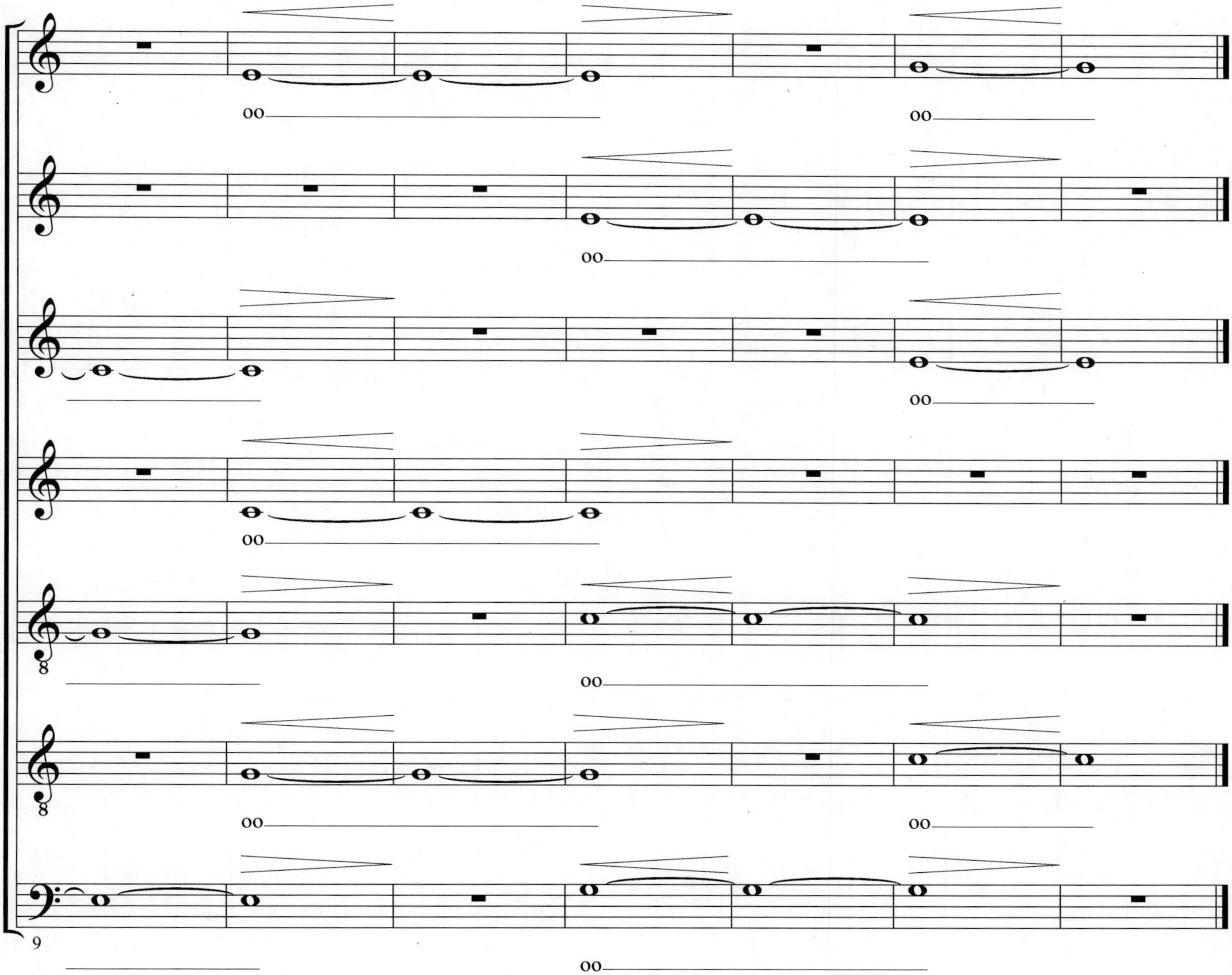

oo
oo
oo
oo
oo
oo
oo
oo
oo
oo

Passing Chord Warm-Up

In three part parallel harmony singing there are chords that align with the key of the song and there are passing chords, built around the passing notes in the melody. These passing chords need to be in tune just as much as the primary chords in each measure, but shouldn't be overemphasized or overthought. This excerpt from the bilingual song "Wo Ai Ni" ("I love you" in Mandarin Chinese), originally recorded on the House Jacks album "Pollen," is an opportunity to work on aligning every chord.

Skills: Intonation, Balance

Whoa, whoa, whoa, whoa whoa, Wo ai
Whoa, whoa, whoa, whoa whoa, Wo ai
Whoa, whoa, whoa, whoa whoa, Wo ai
7
dm dm duh duh dm dm duh dm dm dm dm dm
(Last time end here)
ni Oo Wo ai ni
ni Oo Wo ai ni
ni Oo Wo ai ni
10
dm dm duh dm dm dm dm duh dm dm dm duh

Pop Anticipations Warm-up (Whatchaever Done)

Even harder than singing anticipations in succession is singing an anticipation after singing several straight rhythms. This little ditty sets up the expectation of landing on the beat and then jumps the downbeat, which is deceptively challenging. Practice this with a metronome until your group can sing it without losing time. Singers may find it helpful to physicalize the rhythm (tapped toe, etc) to create an internal metronome.

Skills: Rhythm

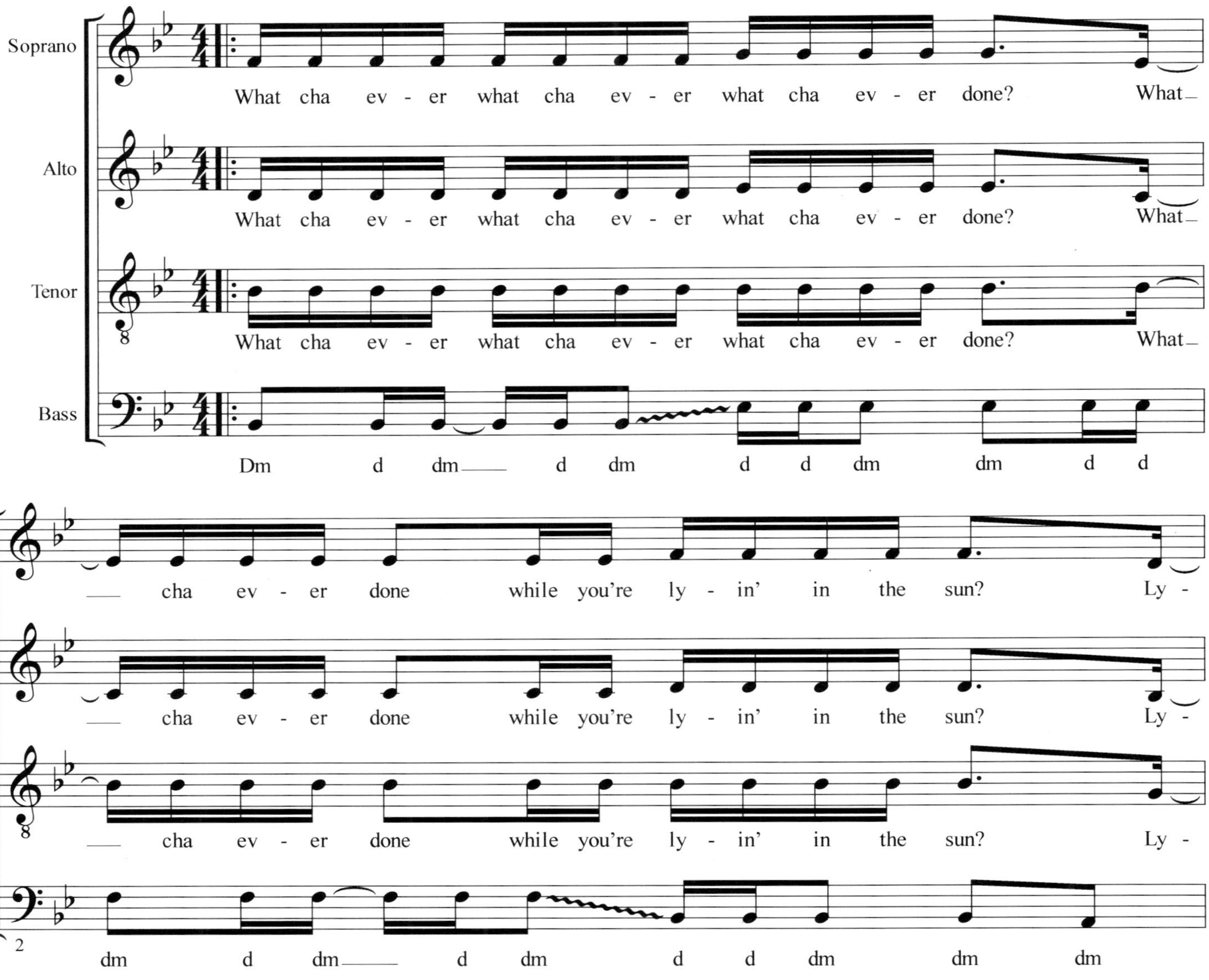

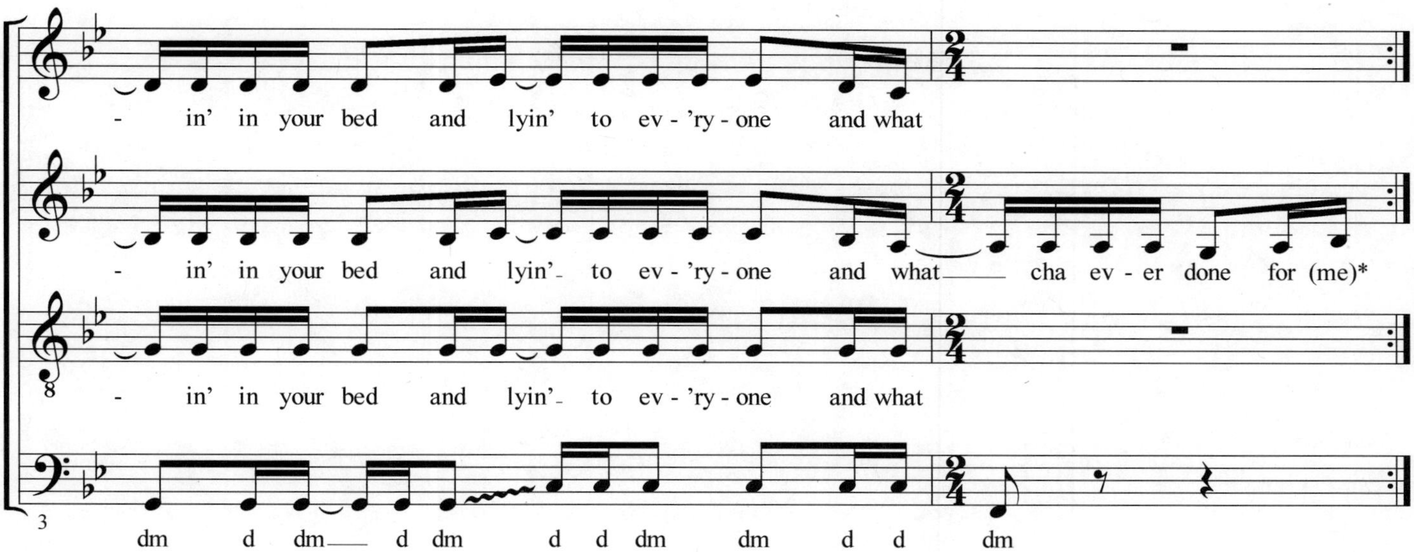

**The word "me" should only be sung the last time.*

R&B Ballad Warm-up

The predominant style of a cappella in the early 1990s was typified by Boyz II Men: a hybrid of modern R&B stylings and more traditional street corner/doo-wop idioms. This warm-up is about more than simply singing in tune, it's a chance for your group to find the music within the notes: Which notes do you emphasize? How should the dynamics ebb and flow? Where should you swoop, where should you add vibrato? Consider this a coloring book: you choose which colors to use, and know that you don't have to color within the lines (you can change anything: notes, rhythms, etc).

Skills: Dynamics, Tone, Improvisation

SHIFTING FOCUS WARM-UP (ATHENA)

Much as is the case in one of Byrd's masses or Bach's fugues, it's important for contemporary a cappella singers to "mix" themselves, especially when the melodic focus shifts from part to part. This song, on The House Jacks album "Fitchy & Grikko," requires singers to constantly listen to how their vocal lines intersect with other parts, both emphasizing and deemphasizing when appropriate.

Skills: Blend, Balance, Dynamics

Ev - 'ry - one wants to know her
Ev - 'ry - one wants to know a the na
Ev - 'ry - one wants a the na
5
duh duh duh duh duh duh duh duh duh duh duh duh duh duh duh duh
Why can't I be the guy?
Why can't I be the guy?
Why can't I be the guy?
7
duh duh duh duh duh duh duh duh duh duh duh

SOUNDCHECK

This isn't so much a warm-up as a short repeated song that The House Jacks used to sing during every warm-up, to give our sound man a consistent song he could use to help balance our levels and eq, and we on stage could use to gauge the monitors. "Get-tin it in deh" was our way of saying "Getting it in there" as in getting it done. As for the reason we sang "Sound check" during the song itself, we found ourselves from time to time doing our sound check in front of an audience, be it outdoors at a state fair, or on a festival stage just before our set. This way the audience clearly new the show hadn't started yet and understood why we were wandering around looking at the monitors as we stopped and started (the rests in the arrangement also gave us a chance to listen to the other parts and/or make comments to the engineers without stopping the song).

Skills: Rhythm, Pitch

Get-tin' it in deh Get-tin' it in deh
Get-tin' it in deh Get-tin' it in deh
Get-tin' it in deh Get-tin' it in deh
5
bum bum bank bank bum bum buh bum bum bank bank bum bum buh
Sound Check Dih vuh nih nit dih vuh nih nit dih vuh nih nit dih vit dih vit
Sound Check Dih vuh nih nit dih vuh nih nit dih vuh nih nit dih vit dih vit
Sound Check
7
bum bum bank bank bum bum buh bum bum bank bank bum bum buh
Ah
Ah
Ah
9
bum bum bank bank bum bum buh bum bum bank bank bum bum buh

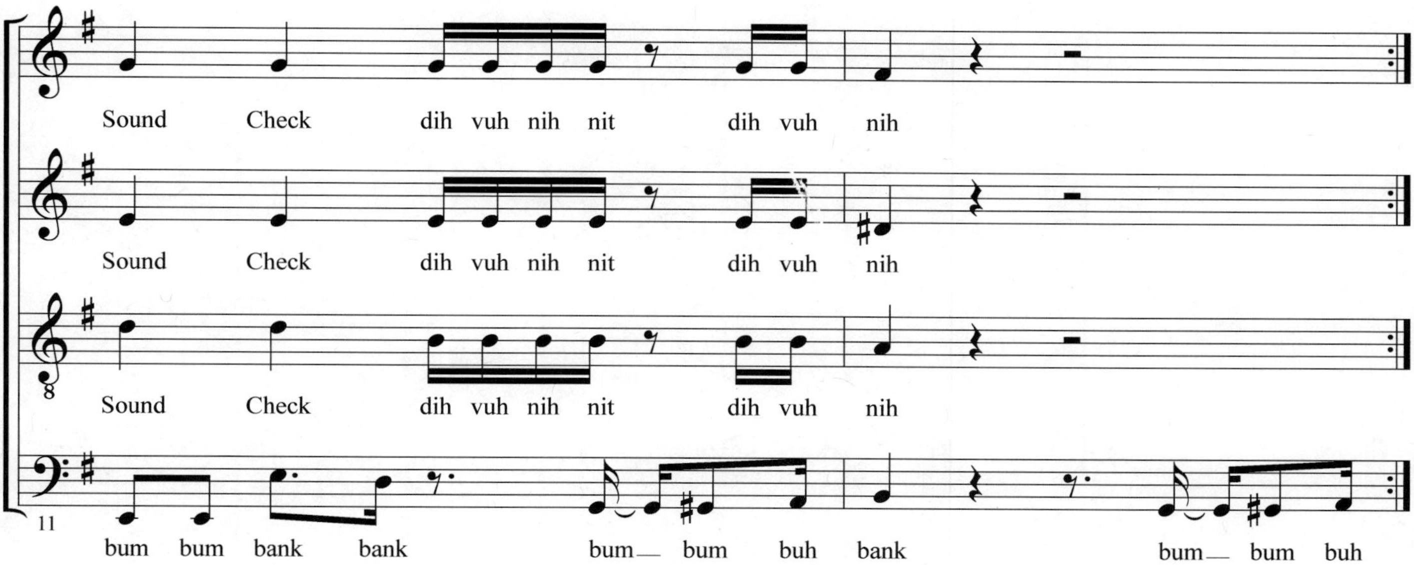

SWOOPING/SCOOPING WARM-UP (THE WAY IT MAKES ME FEEL)

One of The House Jacks most popular songs in the early days (can be found on the albums "Naked Noise," "Funkwich" and "Good Things"), this chorus is an example of "singing in the cracks" as much of the time is spent sliding between chords. Start by learning the notes as written, then practice sliding as a cohesive three-part unit, maintaining relative balance and tuning as you move from note to note. Feel free to follow the various placement of scoops in the recording, or choose your own.

Skills: Balance, Intonation, Rhythm

The way it makes me feel
The way The way that it way that it way that it way that it
The way it makes me feel
3
buh dm buh dm buh dm bum bum bum bum b b b bum
The way it makes me feel
makes me feel way it makes me feel
The way it makes me feel The way it makes me feel
5
buh dm buh dm buh dm bum bum bum bum b b b bum
The way it makes me feel
The way it makes me feel
The way it makes me feel
7
buh dm buh dm buh dm bum bum bum bum b b b bum

Tango: Harmony to Unison Warm-up

Based on the world's most famous Tango – "La Cumparsita" – this warm-up focuses on the transition from harmony to unisons, and to make it additionally challenging, the harmony sections are on a quiet "thm" syllable (like a pizzicato string) whereas the unison, which will undoubtedly be too loud until your singers learn to pull back when joining others, are on a wide open "ah" vowel. Moreover, it's placed where all of your singers will have to navigate register shifts, moving over their break ideally without anyone hearing a difference.

Skills: Tone, Syllables, Dynamics

thum thum thum thum ya da da da da thum thum thum thum
thum thum thum thum ya da da da da thum thum thum thum
thum thum thum thum ya da da da da thum thum thum thum
run dun dun dun drrrr run dun dun dun drrrr run dun dun dun drrrr
7
dom dom dom dom dom dom dom dom
ya da da da da thum thum thum thum ya da da da da
ya da da da da thum thum thum thum ya da da da da
ya da da da da thum thum thum thum ya da da da da
run dun dun dun drrrr run dun dun dun drrrr run dun dun dun drrrr
10
dom dom dom dom dom dom dom dom dom dom

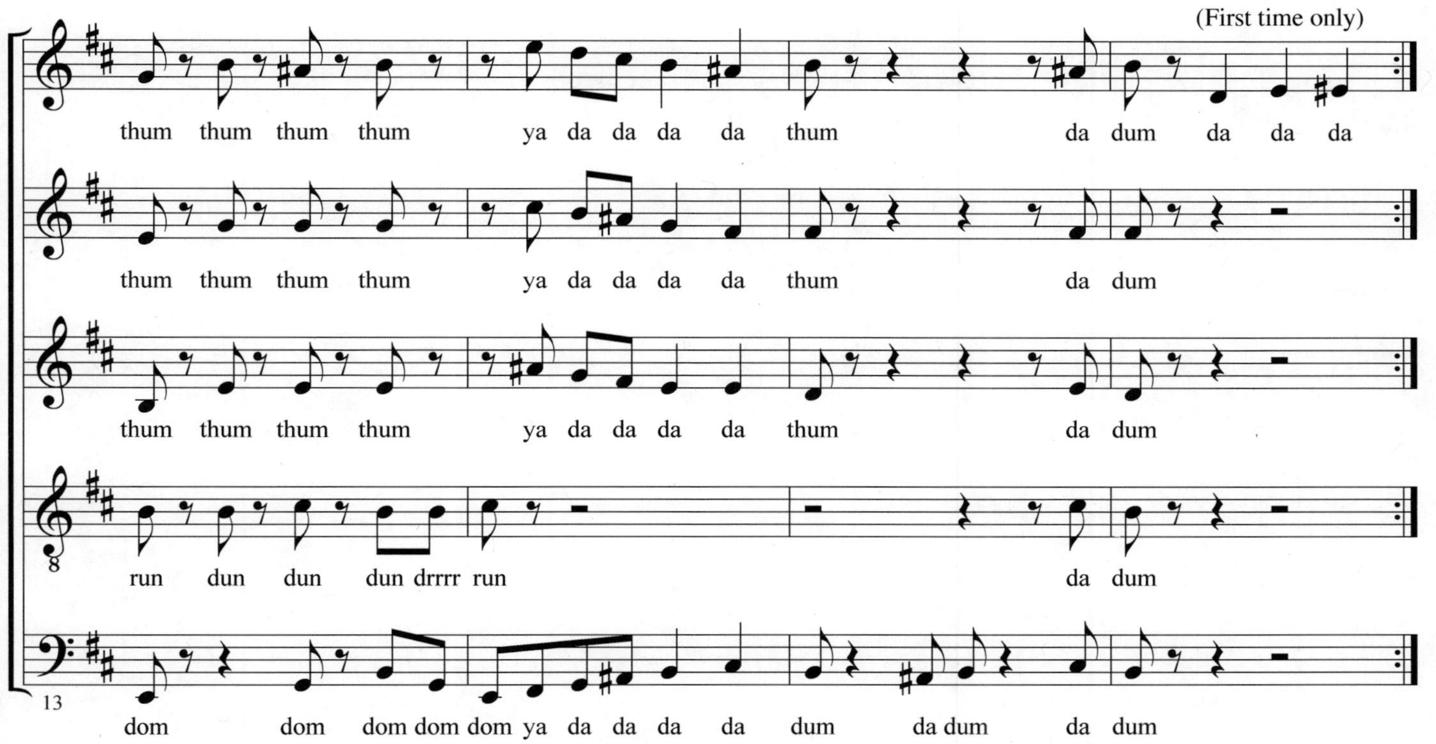
(First time only)
thum thum thum thum ya da da da da thum da dum da da da
thum thum thum thum ya da da da da thum da dum
thum thum thum thum ya da da da da thum da dum
run dun dun dun drrrr run da dum
13
dom dom dom dom dom ya da da da da dum da dum da dum

Tempo Finding Warm-Up (Go Tell It on the Mountain)

Since our bodies are our instrument, we are subject to many variables (weather, mood, time of day) that can affect our performance, especially tempo. This warm-up comes in two sections: slow and fast. Sing each, find the tempi that feel right during a specific time of day, and sing the song later comparing the two. Once you've learned how much a tempo can vary, choose one that you would like to use for each section, then attempt to sing it in all circumstances/environments. (Have one of your singers count off the beginning, then don't direct, and see if where they land on the second tempo naturally.)

Skills: Rhythm

Fast Gospel
mou - hou - n - tain that Je - sus Christ is born!
mou - hou - n - tain that Je - sus Christ is born!
mou - hou - n - tain that Je - sus Christ is born!
dm d d d dm dm dm dm dm dm dm d d Go dm tm dm tm dm tm dm tm
Go tell it on the mount - ain
Go tell it tell it on the moun - tain
Go tell it tell it on the moun - tain
dm tm dm tm dm tm dm tm dm tm dm tm dm tm dm tm dm tm dm tm dm tm dm tm
o - ver the hills and ev - 'ry - where tell it on the
o - ver the hills and ev - 'ry - where tell it on the
o - ver the hills and ev - 'ry - where tell it on the
dm tm dm tm dm tm dm tm dm tm dm tm dm tm dm tm dm tm dm tm dm tm dm tm

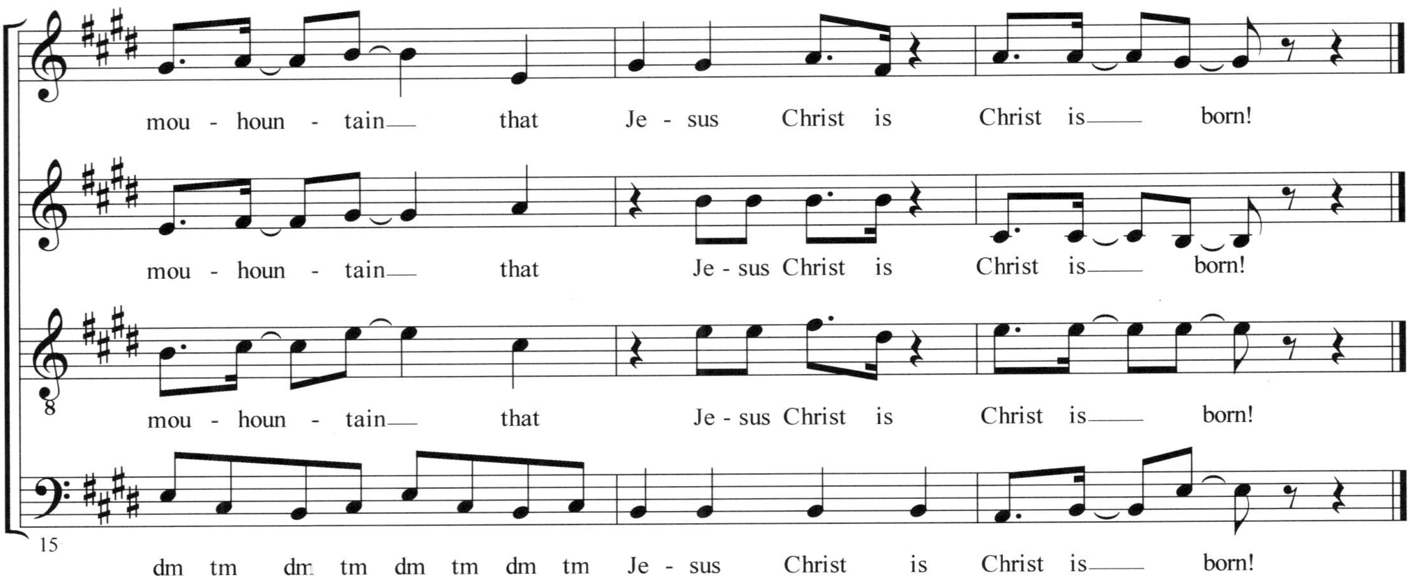

Three Against Two Warm-up

Three against two occurs often in various popular music idioms. Indeed, it's a false three against two as in the first four measures below (two dotted quarters followed by a quarter, an approximated triplet while still remaining in rhythm) or a true hemiola as in the second four measures (which has to occur four times before it "wraps around" and aligns again). The tendency will be to rush the three figure, as it "feels" as though it should be faster than it is. Rehearse this with a metronome if you find the upper voices and bass aren't aligning.

Skills: Rhythm

nuh nuh nuh nuh nuh nuh nuh
nuh nuh nuh nuh nuh nuh nuh
nuh nuh nuh nuh nuh nuh nuh
3
dun dun dun dun dun dun dun dun dun dun dun dun dun dun dun dun
Na na na na na na na na
Na na na na na na na na
Na na na na na na na na
5
Da ba dih da da ba dih da da ba dih dah da ba dih da da ba dih da da ba da ba
na na na na na na na na
na na na na na na na na
na na na na na na na na
7
da ba dih da da ba dih da da ba dih dah da ba dih da da ba dih da da ba da ba

TWO CHORD IMPROV WARM-UP (UH-UH)

Improvisation is a daunting prospect to some singers who have been taught that music is something you should learn from a page. We all make up little songs in our heads from time to time, and improvise in other aspects of our lives freely, so musical improvisation shouldn't be a daunting prospect. This little ditty (written for the film "The Lost Art of Tea Tossing," available on the House Jacks album "BlackJack") is a simple two-chord repeated pattern in the pop style over which singers new to the concept of vocal improv can begin to spread their wings. Start with simple tasks: one note over the entire form, followed by one note per measure, one pitch with a varying rhythm, and so on.

Skills: Improvisation

uh uh
n no no no n no n no n no no no no no!
n no no no n no n no n no no no no no!
n no no no n no n no n no no no no no!

Vocal Percussion Jam

Rather than being definitive, the following four measure patterns are presented simply to get your group started on the road to a different vocal percussion jam every time you meet. You can choose any tempo, feel, and combination of instrumental and vocal sounds, some pitched, some purely percussive. The only rules we recommend are 1) add parts one by one so people can listen and create complimentary rhythms; 2) consistent rhythm is more important than any specific sound or tone; and 3) once established, only vary each pattern slightly, lest the entire jam session become an incoherent mess. Less is more.

Skills: Vocal Percussion

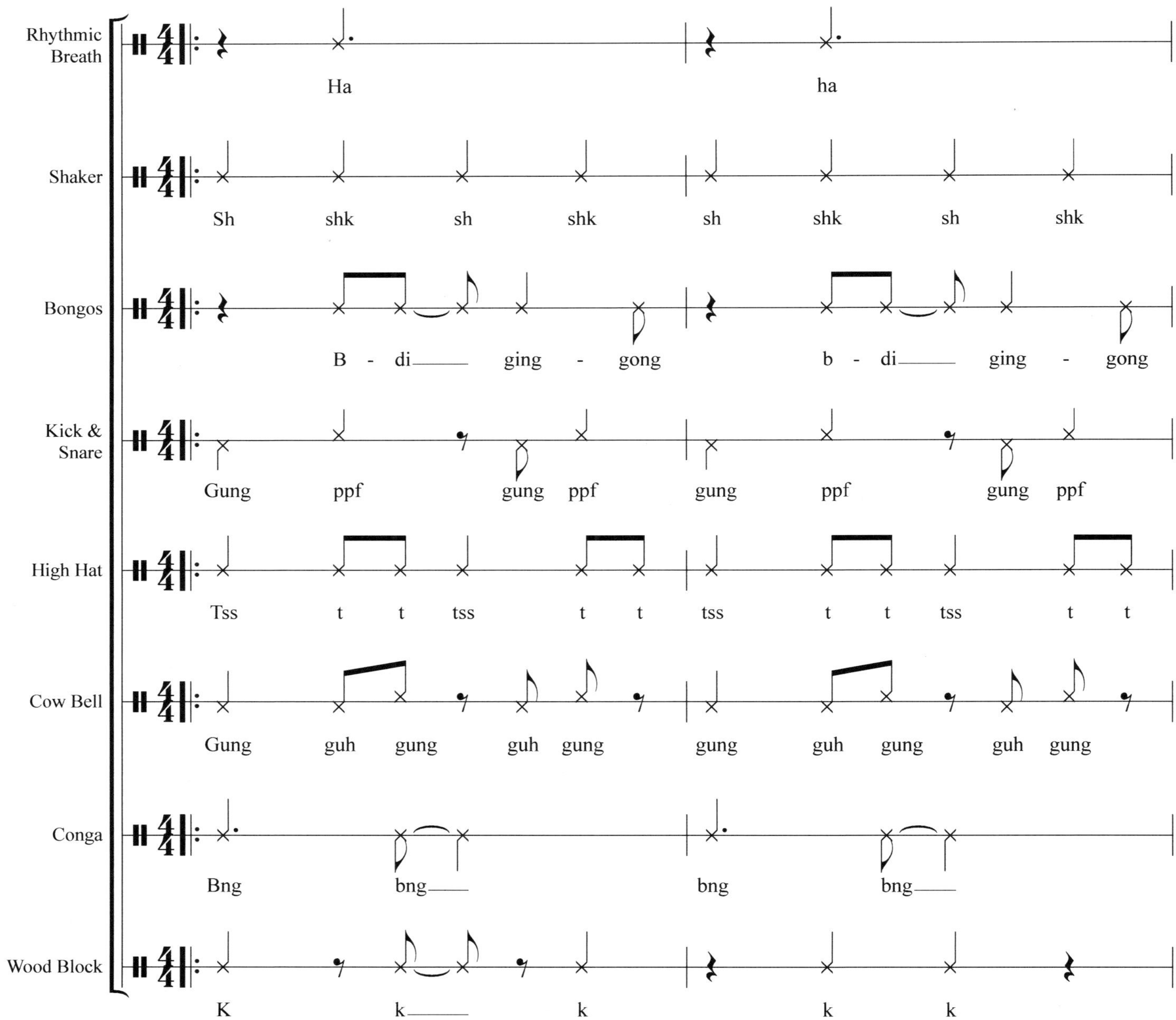

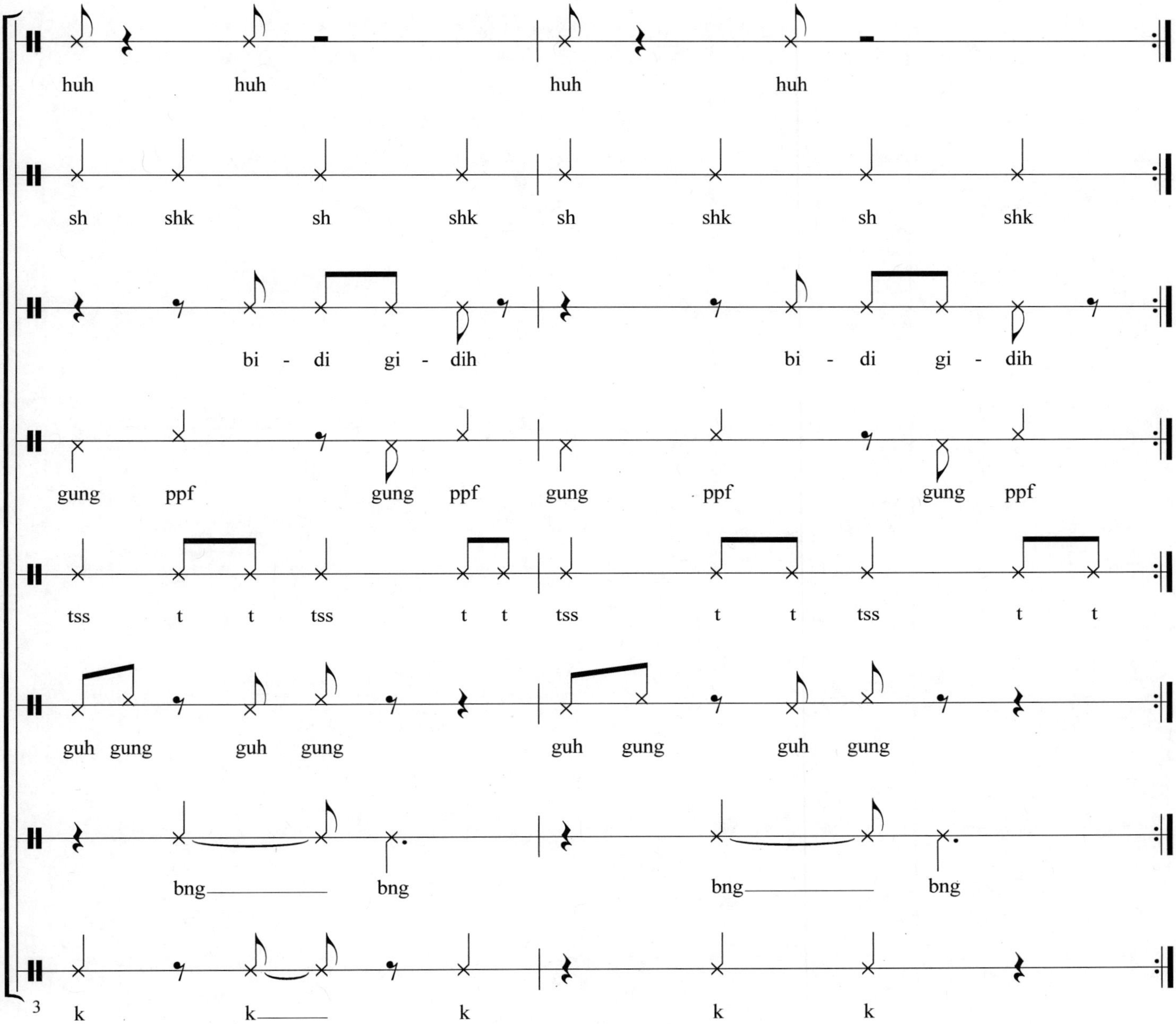
huh huh huh huh
sh shk sh shk sh shk sh shk
bi - di gi - dih bi - di gi - dih
gung ppf gung ppf gung ppf gung ppf
tss t t tss t t tss t t tss t t
guh gung guh gung guh gung guh gung
bng bng bng bng
3
k k k k k

Jazz

THREE-PART ALIGNMENT WARM-UP

One of the first challenges new a cappella singers face is learning how to align with other vocal parts even though they're singing completely different rhythms and syllables. Start with one part, get that locked into a good groove, then add the second part, and when those two are locked, add the third. Once you have this mastered, have your singers create their own interlocking patterns: one person in a section improvises a part, the section joins him/her, then another, etc.

Skills: Rhythm, Improvisation

Three-Part Leap into Dissonance Warm-Up

We're drawn to the sound of complex chords on the piano because they're effortless, always in tune. Dissonances in vocal music are far more difficult because our voices are "fretless" and do not effortlessly strike the same note every time, especially when surrounded by other notes that tell our ear "this pitch is wrong!" Even more challenging is to approach these harmonies from a distance, with a leap. Listen to this exercise on the piano, then replicate with voices. You'll find singing with less vibrato will help.

Skills: Intervals, Intonation, Tone

Bossa Nova Warm-up (Quiet Moon)

One of my personal favorite styles of music, Bossa Nova is a gentle blend of complex harmonies and rhythmic textures. This excerpt from the song "Quiet Moon" (from The House Jacks' album "Pollen") can be sung with or without the melody line, and makes a good bed for more advanced vocal improvisers (as the complex chord progression changes each measure). For an even greater challenge, have two people improvise over this texture, trading back and forth, each building on the musical ideas of the person before.

Skills: Improvisation, Rhythm

dm dm dm dm dm dm dm dm
dm dm dm dm dm dm dm dm
dm dm dm dm dm dm dm dm
7
dm dm dm dm dm dm dm dm dm
Let's go down
dm dm dm dm dm dm dm
dm dm dm dm dm dm dm
dm dm dm dm dm dm dm
11
dm dm dm dm dm dm dm dm

Close Harmony Chord Balancing Warm-Up (Down and Out)

Vocal jazz writing often includes homophonic, close-voiced moving parts in 4 parts, which results in a number of 6ths, 7ths and 9ths being added to triads in rapid succession. The key to balancing these chords is to know when you're on a primary chord factor and when you're on a color note. This passage offers an opportunity for your singers to practice this note-by-note rebalancing. When singing, prepare the singers to freeze and hold chords, listening to and rebalancing the chord factors if they're not locking.

Skills: Intonation, Intervals, Blend, Balance

dat da Sing - in' and swing - in', yeah, in har - mo - ny.
dat da Sing - in' and swing - in', yeah, in har - mo - ny.
dat da Sing - in' and swing - in', yeah, in har - mo - ny.
8
dat da Sing - in' and swing - in', yeah, in har - mo - ny.
6
dm tm dm ba tm ba dm dm tm dm tm
Sing - in' amd swing - in', yeah, in har - mo - ny.
Sing - in' amd swing - in', yeah, in har - mo - ny.
Sing - in' amd swing - in', yeah, in har - mo - ny.
8
Sing - in' amd swing - in', yeah, in har - mo - ny.
9
dm tm dm tm dm ba tm dm ba dm ba

Funk Anticipations Warm-up

Popular music has grown increasingly rhythmic over the past century, and the public's ear has embraced more complexity. As a result, singers now are called upon to create intricate patterns with their voices, which sometime goes against their natural instincts. Anticipations present a particular problem for young singers, as the universal tendency to rush fast anticipated rhythms results in a lost groove, especially when not supported by a strong rhythm section. Sing this exercise with a metronome initially and perhaps later a vocal percussionist so your singers can hear how they want to rush and learn to counteract this by internalizing the downbeat.

Skills: Rhythm, Intervals

Yeah yeah na na na ba ba ba ba ba dap
Yeah yeah ba ba ba ba ba dap
Yeah yeah ba ba ba ba ba dap
5
dum buh dum buh dum buh duh dum buh dum buh duh duh duh duh duh duh
yeah yeah na na na ba ba ba ba ba dap
yeah yeah na na na ba ba ba ba ba dap
yeah yeah na na na ba ba ba ba ba dap
7
dum buh dum buh dum buh duh dum buh dum buh buh buh

Gospel Improv Warm-up

There is no emotion that a cappella more powerfully and convincingly expresses than joy: the joy of singing, the joy of creating, the joy of friendship and community. This passage, taken from the breakdown/chant section of a classic gospel tune, is an opportunity for your singers to both work on their improvisational skills, and consistently tap into their deep well of joy when singing. If singing with consistent emotion is challenging for your group, I have written a book on this very topic: "The Heart of Vocal Harmony."

Skills: Rhythm, Pitch, Improvisation

oh hap - py hap - py day oh hap - py hap - py day
day down down down down down day down down down hap - py
day down down down down down day down down down hap - py
day down down down down down day down down down hap - py
d d da da da da da da da da da da da da da da da
5
hap - py day yeah
day down down down down down day down down down hap - py way yeah!
day down down down down down day down down down hap - py way yeah!
day down down down down down day down down down hap - py way yeah!
d d da da da da da da da da da da da da da da da way yeah!
7

Gospel Warm-up

This warm-up should start at a moderate tempo, as each time you repeat it you should both move up a half step, and speed the song up. After a couple full passes, you can repeat back to just the chorus (measure 11), which will increase the rate of modulations. The key to Gospel music is passion, and you'll find this warm-up sounds stiff if it's sung without energy and joy. Once your singers are engaged and you start accelerating, the key is to keep it full of intensity without getting sloppy.

Skills: Pitch, Rhythm

Nuh nuh nuh nuh oh oh
Nuh nuh nuh nuh oh oh
nuh nuh nuh nuh nuh nuh nuh nuh nuh nuh nuh
6
dm dm dm dm dm dm dm dm dm dm dm dm dm dm dm dm dm dm dm dm dm dm dm dm
nuh nuh nuh nuh nuh nuh Na na na na
nuh nuh nuh nuh nuh nuh Na na na na
nuh nuh nuh nuh nuh nuh Na na na na na na na na na na na na
9
dm dm dm dm dm dm dm dm dm dm dm dm dm dm dm dm dm dm dm dm dm
na na na na Oh
na na na na Oh
na na na na na na na na na na na na na na na na na na na Ba da
12
dm dm dm dm dm dm dm dm dm dm dm dm dm dm dm dm dm dm dm dm

Ba dap ba ba dap ba ba dap ba da da Oh
Ba dap ba ba dap ba ba dap ba da da Oh
ba dap ba ba dap ba ba dap ba da da Na na na na na na na na na na na
dm dm dm dm dm dm dm dm dm dm dm dm
15
1
2
(in appropriate key)
na na na na hoo na na na na
na na na na hoo na na na na
na na na na nuh nuh na na na na
dm dm dm dm dm dm dm dm dm dm dm
18

Jazz/Blues Warm-up

Some warm-ups become group standards as this one did for "American Vybe" at Disney World's Epcot Center
(1999-2005). The singers would take turns improvising solos over the form, sometimes scatting and sometimes singing the blues about their current condition (often humorously complaining about modern living). If you have singers who are shy about scatting, have them start with one note – the tonic – repeating it over this pattern with various rhythms, building to a second note, and so on. In time your whole group will look forward to singing the blues at the beginning of rehearsal. Note: It takes a little time for singers to get used to the sound of a sharp 9 chord, but once they lock it in, they'll always have it.

Skills: Pitch, Intonation, Rhythm, Solo

Sing the cycle once with lyrics (change day of week), then repeat as desired on "doo" while individuals improvise the blues about their day, then end with one final cycle on the lyric

new blues blues you choose choose your blues
dat doo doo doo doo doot doo doo
new blues blues you choose choose your blues
dat doo doo doo doo doot doo doo
7
repeat as desired
choose your blues who's blues? you's blues
doot doo doo who's blues? you's blues
choose your blues who's blues? you's blues
doot doo doo who's blues? you's blues
10
last time:
yeah
yeah
13
dm yeah

Meet the Band

As much a performance piece as a warm-up, this song was written for and performed by The House Jacks for over a decade, one of the most popular songs in our set, as it gave every person an opportunity to solo, be it a scat solo, vocal trumpet solo, vocal bass solo, vocal percussion solo, etc. One person should announce the coming solo during the chorus section, and the various verse/improv sections can be repeated if you'd like longer solos. Basically think of it modularly: put these sections together in any order you'd like, as a warm-up or song in your set.

Skills: Improvisation, Solo, Balance, Vocal Percussion

3
Meet the band meet the band meet it meet it
Meet the band meet the band meet it meet it
Meet the band meet the band meet it meet it
6
bm bm bm bm bm bm buh duh duh duh duh
Verse/Improv Section
Meet the band meet the band meet the band
Meet the band meet the band meet the band
Meet the band meet the band meet the band
8
Bm bm bm bm b bm bm bm bm b bm bm bm bm b
meet the band meet the band meet the band meet the band meet it meet it
meet the band meet the band meet the band meet the band meet it meet it
meet the band meet the band meet the band meet the band meet it meet it
11
bm bm bm bm b bm bm bm bm bm bm buh duh duh duh duh

Alternate Verse
Meet the band meet the band meet the band
Meet the band meet the band meet the band
Meet the band meet the band meet the band
Bm bm bm bm b bm bm bm bm b bm bm bm bm b
14
Meet the band the band the band meet the band meet the
Meet the band the band the band meet the band meet the
Meet the band the band the band meet the band meet the
bm bm bm bm b bm bm bm bm bm bm buh duh duh duh duh
17
Bass Solo Verse
Oh
Oh
Oh
20

Dm dm dm meet it meet it meet it
Dm dm dm meet it meet it meet it
Dm dm dm meet it meet it meet it
24
Percussion Solo Verse
Oh meet the band oh meet the band
Oh meet the band oh meet the band
26
the band the band meet it meet it meet it
the band the band meet it meet it meet it
30

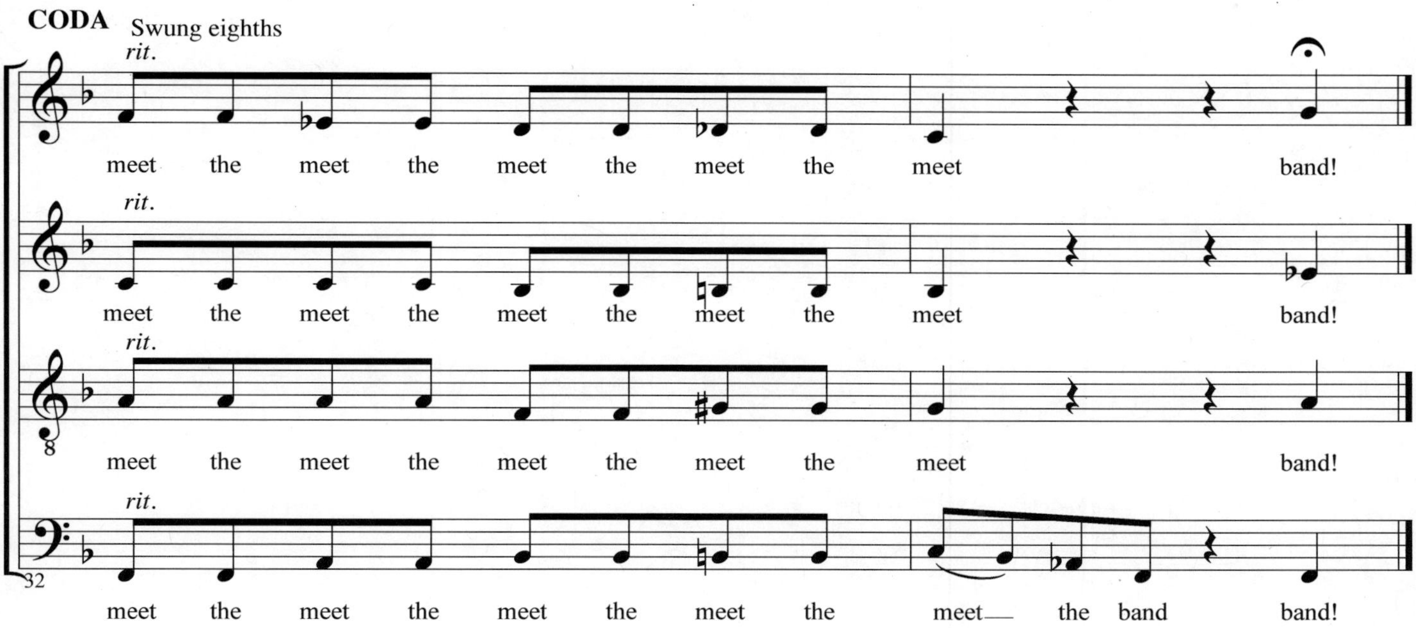

SWING ERA WARM-UP (ANTS IN THE KITCHEN)

That classic 1940's Andrews Sisters/Radio Hour close harmony sound is the result of perfectly aligned vowels and rhythms, moving together in rapid succession, like the Blue Angels flying in perfect formation. This little ditty written for a political movie (can be heard on The House Jacks album "BlackJack") is an opportunity to recreate that classic swing era sound: first make it incredibly precise, then through repetition keep the tightness while working in a measure of looseness so that it sounds effortless.

Skills: Rhythm, Blend, Balance

you got - ta block all the holes
If ya don't want ants in the
you got - ta block all the holes
If ya don't want ants in the
you got - ta block all the holes
If ya don't want ants in the
thum thum thumthumthum thum thum thum thum
kitch - en
you got - ta block 'em all
you got ta block 'em up
kitch - en
you got - ta block 'em all
you got ta block 'em up
kitch - en
you got - ta block 'em all
you got ta block 'em up
thum thum thum thum thum thum
you got - ta block all the holes
If ya
yeah!
you got - ta block all the holes
If ya
yeah!
you got - ta block all the holes
If ya
yeah!
thum thum thum thum
block all the holes
block all the holes

ABOUT THE AUTHORS

"The father of contemporary a cappella" – Entertainment Weekly

"A one man a cappella revolution" – Boston Globe

"Deke Sharon makes a cappella cool again" – NPR

DEKE SHARON

Born in San Francisco, California, Deke Sharon has been performing professionally since the age of 8, and as a child toured North America and shared the stage in operas with the likes of Pavarotti. Heralded as "The Father of Contemporary A Cappella," he is responsible for the current sound of modern a cappella, having pioneered the modern vocal-instrumental sound in college, subsequently spreading it around the world. He produced "The Sing-Off" on NBC and worldwide (Netherlands, China, South Africa). In addition, Deke served as arranger, on-site music director and vocal producer for Universal's "Pitch Perfect" 1, 2 & 3 starring Anna Kendrick & Rebel Wilson.

Deke founded the Contemporary A Cappella Society while in college, and is responsible for many seminal a cappella programs, including the CARAs (Contemporary A Cappella Recording Awards), ICCAs (International Championship of College A Cappella), BOCA (Best of College A Cappella Compilation), the first contemporary a cappella conferences (the A Cappella Summit), the Contemporary A Cappella League, the professional theatrical touring ensemble Vocalosity, and Camp A Cappella. He is also contemporary cappella's most prolific arranger, having arranged over 2,000 songs, with many of them in print worldwide with Hal Leonard/Contemporary A Cappella Publishing. He has written 5 books: "Acappella Arranging" (2012), "A Cappella" (2015) and "The Heart of Vocal Harmony" (2016), "A Cappella Warm-ups for Pop and Jazz Choir (2017) and "So You Want To Sing A Cappella (2017). He is also vocal arranger and producer for the Broadway's first a cappella musical: In Transit (2016).

As the founder, director and arranger for the House Jacks for 24 years, the original "Rock Band Without Instruments," Deke shared the stage with countless music legends, including Ray Charles, James Brown, Crosby Stills and Nash, Run DMC, The Temptations, LL Cool J and the Four Tops, performed for luminaries including President Bill Clinton and performed the Monday Night Football Theme with Hank Williams Jr. in 2011. He has produced dozens of award winning a cappella albums (including Straight No Chaser, Committed, Nota, Street Corner Symphony and the Tufts Beelzebubs, Pitch Perfect and In Transit), created a cappella groups for Disneyland and Disneyworld, and frequently tours the world teaching a variety of topics to students and professional singers. His voice can be heard in commercials and video games, including "Just Dance Kids 2." He is one of only 20 honorary members of the Barbershop Harmony Society since 1938, as well as an honorary member of BYU Vocal Point, and received CASA's lifetime achievement award in 2016 and the Tufts Barnum Award for excellence in entertainment in 2017. You can see him on television on Lifetime's "Pitch Slapped" (2016) and his newest show for the BBC: "Pitch Battle" or online at www.dekesharon.com.

J.D. Frizzell, a composer, conductor, and baritone, is the Director of Fine Arts and Director of Vocal Music at Briarcrest Christian School in Memphis, TN. He earned his Doctor of Musical Arts Degree in Choral Conducting degree from The University of Kentucky. Dr. Frizzell earned the double Master's in Music Theory/Composition and Conducting from The University of Southern Mississippi, where he also earned the bachelor's degree in Music History and Literature.

Dr. Frizzell, winner of the 2007 Intégrales Composition Contest, writes music for choir, orchestra, symphonic band, voice, handbells, chamber ensembles, and solo instruments. With music published by many major publishing houses, he has had best sellers throughout the world. Frizzell was chosen by the board of the Tennessee Music Educators Association as the 2011 Outstanding Young Music Educator. Additionally, he was awarded the Dr. Clair E. Cox Award for Teaching Excellence.

As the Director of Fine Arts at Briarcrest, Dr. Frizzell leads a faculty of twelve full time faculty-artists and is responsible for coordinating curriculum, instruction, and budgets for all of the fine arts programs (K2-12th grade). He also serves as an advocate and school liaison for all of the visual art, instrumental music, vocal music, dance, theatre, and technical production programs. As the Director of Vocal Music, he teaches the Concert Choir, Chamber Choir, and OneVoice. Additionally, Dr. Frizzell works with the middle and elementary school choirs when needed.

A leader in the contemporary a cappella movement, he is the co-founder and President of The A Cappella Education Association, a nonprofit dedicated to helping groups around the world. His high school a cappella group, OneVoice, is a SONY Recording Artist. They were the winners of the Macy's A Cappella Challenge judged by Pentatonix and contestants on America's Got Talent. Frizzell is also the Director of Education and Marketing for Camp A Cappella.

Dr. Frizzell is active as a presenter, adjudicator, clinician, and guest conductor. As an active member of TNMEA, NATS, ACDA, and WTVMEA, he has served in multiple volunteer capacities, including two-time Chairperson of All-West Honor Choir Auditions and Performances and Choral Festival. He is also the Southern Division ACDA R & S Chair for Men's Choirs. The board of the Cystic Fibrosis Foundation named him one of "Memphis' Finest" for his philanthropic efforts. He lives in Memphis, TN with his wife, Emily, son, Henry, and dogs, Sally and Ari.

For commission, conducting, workshop, or other booking information, please visit www.jdfrizzell.com.